Eamon Evans is the author of fifteen books, one or two of them pretty good. He's written about history, sport, scandals, words, films, alcohol and urban legends, but until *The Importance of Being Miserable* he's not done much with his philosophy degree, apart from bore people at parties. Eamon lives with his family in Melbourne, where he writes, teaches, overwaters his garden and worries about going bald.

THE IMPORTANCE
of BEING
MISERABLE

EAMON EVANS

affirm
press

First published in Australia in 2026 by Affirm Press,
a Simon & Schuster (Australia) Pty Limited company
Wurundjeri Woiwurrung Country
Level 3, 162 Collins Street, Melbourne VIC 3000

Affirm Press is located on the unceded land of the Wurundjeri Woiwurrung peoples
of the Kulin Nation. Affirm Press pays respect to their Elders past and present.

New York Amsterdam/Antwerp London Toronto Sydney/Melbourne New Delhi
Visit our website at www.simonandschuster.com.au

AFFIRM PRESS and design are trademarks of Affirm Press Pty
Ltd, Inc., used under licence by Simon & Schuster, LLC.

10 9 8 7 6 5 4 3 2 1

A catalogue record for this
book is available from the
National Library of Australia

9781923135192 (paperback)
9781761639753 (ebook)

Cover design by Josh Durham/Design by Committee
Cover images: donkey by unorobus.gmail.com/depositphotos.com;
Rodin's *The Thinker* courtesy of iStock
Typeset by Post Pre-press Group in 12.5/18 pt Garamond Premier Pro
Printed and bound in Australia by the Opus Group

MIX
Paper from
responsible sources
FSC® C001695

To Matt Lennox, who once said,
'No offence, but who the hell is going to read this?'
May this dedication help him to get past page one.

CONTENTS

INTRODUCTION

SHINY HAPPY PEOPLE

Why the gospel of joy might just be a scam

All his life – the office on the docks, his room and
his nights of sleep there, the restaurant he went to,
his mistress – he had pursued single-mindedly a
happiness which in his heart he believed was impossible.
In this he was no different from anyone else.

Albert Camus, *A Happy Death*, 1971

Do you know Nietzsche? First name: Friedrich? He was a small German guy with a great, big moustache who spent his days ranting, laughing, ranting some more, dancing about naked and battling syphilis. Before finally being carted off to a mental asylum (after a regrettable incident involving a horse), our hero also enjoyed writing long, dense philosophical tracts about some of the many problems facing Western civilisation.

Chief among them: the decline of religion. 'God is dead,' said Fred, back in 1882. After being kept afloat for thousands of years by their belief in some deity – after centuries of going to church, saying their prayers and thinking and feeling whatever the Bible ordained – the increasingly secular citizens of the West were now drifting towards a sort of cultural shipwreck. Without a God to guide them, they would be rudderless and meander aimlessly along the river of life. And sooner or later, they would sink straight to the bottom after crashing into the rocks of existential despair.

In short, Western civilisation would need to find a new kind of meaning, a new kind of purpose, a new way to make sense of life's chaos.

But it turns out that Nietzsche need not have worried, because in recent years we have done just that. God is not dead; he just has a new name. We now worship at the altar of happiness. Self-help books are the new bibles, therapists the new priests and serotonin the new holy sacrament. At some point in the last century or so, the cultures of the West collectively decided that the purpose of life was for us to enjoy it. For every day to be fulfilling and fun. If someone asks how you are, the correct answer is 'good'.

Do I exaggerate? No, I do not. Happiness is the ending of every movie, the promise of every ad. It's stitched into birthday cards, pumped into kids' shows and baked into corporate wellness policies. It's a rare company that doesn't claim to care about its staff's 'emotional well-being' these days – or at least mention it in a PowerPoint. We eat Happy Meals, pop happy pills, drink at a happy hour and aim to be happy campers. We wish each other happy birthday, happy holidays, happy Hanukkah and happy new year, in between instructions to 'have a good day'.

But it doesn't stop there. We're expected to raise happy children, have happy marriages, smile in every photo and feel passionate about our jobs. Type 'happiness' into Amazon and you'll get more than 200,000 results like *The Happiness Advantage*, *Hardwiring Happiness*, *The Art of Happiness* and *Happiness for Dummies* – all promising to deliver the emotional jackpot. Not to mention all sorts of scented candles, gratitude journals, crystals and courses 100 per cent guaranteed to provide inner peace.

And it's not just the crappy products. Crappy policymakers are flogging happiness too. We now have a World Happiness Report, a Global Happiness Index and Happiness Institutes springing up at universities. Some governments are even trying to find ways to measure 'national well-being' alongside GDP, following Bhutan, where the Gross National Happiness Index was instituted as the goal of the government in its constitution in 2008.

Like all religions, of course, this one can take many forms. Some believers think happiness can be found by starting a family, while for others it involves wealth or fame. Some like fine dining, others a good film. Still more people prefer hiking or heroin. I could go on and on. In fact, I think I will. There's yoga. There's reading. There's music. There's meditation. There's following a sports team or invading Ukraine. From doing good deeds or getting a dog to travelling the world or having a nice cup of tea, there are as many definitions of 'happiness' as there are people pursuing it.

But at heart, we all agree on one thing: life is just too short to be miserable. Happiness is a state we all want to enjoy, all the time and in every way. Our relationships should be passionate, our families should be supportive. Our work should be meaningful, our friends should be fun. Our salaries should be ample, our homes should be stylish. Our bodies should be fit, our food should taste good.

And if we're not happy, then something is wrong. Sadness, frustration and pain are bugs in the system, problems to be solved, a sign that things have not gone according to plan. Because happiness is what we want. To not pursue it is to commit to a slightly weird kind of heresy. For who would ever question the gospel of joy?

Well, it turns out I have an answer to that question. And that answer is 'just about everyone'. It would barely have occurred to our ancestors to treat happiness as a right or a goal. Nobody in 300,000 BCE woke up expecting the universe to cater to their emotional needs. If they got through the day without coughing up blood, on the whole, they were doing just fine.

Today's obsession with happiness is a freak cultural event – a strange, modern quirk that's wildly out of step with 99.9 per cent of all human history. Ever since the first caveman ate a poisonous berry, or touched a fire and thought 'fuck me, that's hot', human beings have more or less accepted that life can be shit. That semi-regular suffering wasn't a bug in the system so much as the system itself. Happiness, for our ancestors, was like a good Australian film. That is, an accident of fate.

And if anything changed around 500 BCE, it was because happiness became an accident that it was good to avoid. For ancient philosophers or medieval Christians, pleasure was something to be suspicious of, a sure sign that a person was a little too frivolous. Or worse, on the road to sin.

This book is the story of when and why the West stopped seeing happiness as an occasional treat and started to see it as a default setting. But above all, it's about when and why we arrived at the crazy conclusion that if we're not feeling happy, something is wrong.

Because here's the thing, folks: sadness isn't a bug in the machine of life. It's an essential cog. It's a vital part of the human experience. And in many ways, it's a great one as well. Feeling miserable is extremely important. Read on if you want to know why.

1

GOLDEN YEARS

Why you can't know light without a little darkness

The intention that man should be happy is not included in the plan of Creation. What we call happiness in the strictest sense comes from the (preferably sudden) satisfaction of needs which have been dammed up to a high degree and it is from its nature only possible as an episodic phenomenon.

Sigmund Freud, *Civilization and Its Discontents*, 1930

Nostalgia is often seen as a harmless indulgence, as something wholesome and sweet and benign. When the future is uncertain and the present slightly sucks, why not slip on some rose-tinted glasses and take a stroll down memory lane? Why not head back to a time when you were *happy*?

Well, I am here to tell you why not. That's the sort of frank and fearless service you will come to expect from this book. Just call me 'Mr Hard Truths'.

The problem with celebrating 'the golden days' is that we are programmed to forget all the ways they were brown. 'Nostalgia,' as some obscure wordsmith once put it, 'is a file that removes the rough edges from the good old days.' It's also been called a 'seductive liar' by another man who could hew a fine phrase

Their point is that days, weeks or years always look better in hindsight, because we tend to forget all the bits that were blah. We remember the BBQs, the parties, the warm sunny days. That time the teacher farted in class. But we conveniently edit out the boredom, the anxiety, the sunburn, the fatigue. The time when the person farting was us. Memory is not a documentary – it's a scripted movie with special effects. Our brains run selected memories through a filter, add some soft lighting and make sure all the actors have make-up.

This is why, deep down, most adults believe that pop culture peaked in their teens, and that 'kids today' just don't 'get it'. Kids have just not been getting it for thousands of years and will keep on not getting it for thousands to come. Here's the inscription on a 4000-year-old Egyptian tomb: 'We live in a decaying age. Young people no longer respect their parents. They are rude and impatient. They frequently inhabit taverns and lack self-control.'

In 700 BCE, Greek poet Hesiod sighed, 'The morals of our youth are in decay.' A few centuries later, Socrates piled on: 'The young people today think of nothing but themselves. They have no respect for parents or elders. They contradict their teachers, chatter before company, gobble their food and tyrannize their teachers.' (Also, girls were apparently 'forward, immodest and unwomanly in speech, behaviour and dress.' So, not a fan.)

Fast-forward to medieval France and priests were saying the same thing, while by the 1650s you had American colonists lamenting the way the 'disobedient and careless' youth of the New World were 'falling into drunkenness, profaneness and disorderly practices'. Even the famously uptight Victorians ran newspaper columns about 'reckless youth' and how 'this new generation is simply awful'. Every era has had its moral panic about the next. The names change. The clothes change. But the eye-rolling stays the same.

But this phenomenon is not just confined to memories of childhood. It extends to our memories of the world. We don't just airbrush our past – we airbrush our memories of history itself. We imagine a simpler, purer, better time. A time when politicians were more noble, jobs were more stable, music was more soulful and service was less shit. A time when children said 'please', celebrities had class, communities really cared and society made sense.

And we've been doing it for forever – and probably for a while before that. Governments, for example, have been going downhill since the Bronze Age. Ancient Greeks complained about taxes. Egyptians moaned about corruption. Romans grumbled that their senators were useless freeloaders who never listened. It was basically Twitter with togas.

The economy? Sure, everything's terrible now, but when exactly was everything fine? Before the current cost-of-living crisis, there was a mass unemployment crisis. Before that, stagflation. Before that, rationing. Before that, the Great Depression. And before that, serfs getting paid in turnips and back pain, cholera and the occasional plague. At no point was there a golden era of affordable housing, let alone avocados for all.

Education, meanwhile, has been in crisis forever. In 1791, Dr Benjamin Rush, a founding father of the US, lamented that modern schooling was 'unmooring children from virtue'. By 1907, folks were scandalised that kids were reading novels instead of Latin. By the 1940s, kids had already 'lost all discipline'. And in the 1950s, television was 'dumbing down the youth'.

For its part, marriage has been 'dying' since at least 1748, when the British statesman Lord Chesterfield complained that young people were 'too lustful, too flippant in affairs of the heart'. In 1895, Canadian writer Grant Allen declared that 'the decay of the home is the doom of the nation', while the *Ladies' Home Journal* weighed in a few decades later with a cover story on 'Why Marriage Is Failing'. The 1960s blamed the pill, the 2000s blamed texting and today it's Tinder's fault.

Music, meanwhile, has been a source of cultural panic ever since someone beat the drum. Mozart was once called vulgar and Stravinsky caused a riot in Paris. Jazz started out as the devil's soundtrack and Elvis's hips threatened civilisation.

And the younger generation has been doomed forever. The 1980s blamed violent movies and heavy metal. The 1990s blamed Game Boys. The 2000s blamed sugary cereals. Now, the phrase 'screen time' pretty much sums up what is wrong with the world.

So here's the miserable truth, my friends. There's no such thing as 'the good old days'; there's only ever been different kinds of okay ones. Whatever your gran's photo album or a cosy period drama might suggest, there was never a golden age where everybody skipped through the flower-strewn path of life in a state of rosy-cheeked bliss. There was never a time when every single person said, 'Well, I'll be jiggered! Look around you, old bean. We've gone and done it. The world is just perfect.' Human beings have always felt pain and boredom, have always been prey to fear, worry and dread.

Constant, widespread 'happiness', in short, has never actually happened. And here's the thing, folks: it never will. The idea that we should be happy all the time sounds fine in theory, like seeing Shakespeare or going camping with kids. But in practice, it's not just difficult – it's completely impossible. A total pipedream.

Why?

Well, think, for a moment, about how we see happiness. While no two people can agree on what it is, we're pretty much united on what it is *not*: misery. Whatever else we might believe about happiness, we're all pretty sure it means not feeling bad. Not feeling sad. Not feeling consumed by fear, worry and dread.

Misery, by this logic, is an obstacle to happiness. An enemy that must be fought and conquered. So far, so good, but there's just one tiny issue with this logic. It is not logical at all. In fact, it's completely ridiculous. Happiness doesn't happen *in spite of* misery; happiness happens *because of* it.

What exactly do I mean by this? Well, have you ever noticed how people always seem to want more, even when they already have plenty? How it wasn't enough for Napoleon to be master of Europe, he had to try to conquer Russia as well? How it wasn't enough for Elon Musk to be one of the world's richest people, he also had to become one of its worst?

But this isn't because some people are prats. It's because the human brain is biologically wired to stay hungry. The more we get, the more we want – and the harder it becomes to feel impressed by anything at all. Fly first class once and suddenly economy feels like a war crime. Spend a few months in a mansion and you'll start eyeing palaces. The extraordinary becomes ordinary. The magic fades. What once dazzled now just ... exists.

Our brains are stunningly adaptable – almost too adaptable. Success doesn't satisfy; it just moves the goalposts. We normalise everything: wealth, tragedy, new shoes, breakups, beachfront views. Your dream job becomes just another line on the CV. Your new house turns out to have dodgy plumbing. That gleaming new car? Within weeks, it's just a metal box with cup holders. Sail around the Mediterranean on a yacht for four years and eventually, you're not euphoric – you're just sunburnt and slightly sick of prosecco.

In the end, your brain keeps trucking along, adjusting its expectations and rewriting your emotional script. As German philosopher Schopenhauer put it, 'Desire is like hunger. The moment it's satisfied, it disappears.' The mouthful of joy vanishes the second it's swallowed, leaving nothing behind but another craving.

And that's what keeps gamblers gambling, 80-year-old rock stars releasing albums and millionaires working 18-hour days when they could be doing anything else (for example, having a nap). If you've ever wondered why Adam Sandler keeps on making shit movies, despite my constant pleas that he please, please, please, *please* just stop, the answer does not just lie in the troubled recesses of his mind. The answer lies in the troubled minds of us all.

So I'm sorry if this comes as slightly bad news, but at the end of the day, it really doesn't matter what you do with your life. It really doesn't matter if you live out your dreams. You could find true love, travel the world, buy a great home and raise lovely kids, but you still won't be fully satisfied. Your pursuit of happiness will never come to an end, because happiness is not designed to be caught. The moment you grasp hold of the thing, it immediately slips out of reach.

But fret not, reader, for I have good news as well. If you ever *did* manage to be 100 per cent happy with your lot, you'd never be truly happy. What do I mean by this? Let me explain.

Try to imagine something 'hot'. A frying pan left on the stove for a few minutes – easy enough. Now imagine you've never felt 'cold'. Never touched an ice block, never shivered through winter, never left the steamy confines of a sauna. Suddenly, 'hot' becomes harder to define. Because without contrast, it loses all meaning. If everything is hot, then nothing is hot. The same goes for cold. Or light and dark. Tall and short. Fat and thin. Wet and dry.

We only understand these things because we've experienced their opposite. And the same applies to the thing we call happiness.

We recognise emotional highs only because we've been through emotional lows. We have mountains because we have valleys.

As American psychologists Shane Frederick and George Loewenstein put it, happiness is 'not an isolated state but a comparative one', a state that 'derives significance from the contrast between states of being'. Joy doesn't happen in spite of sadness. It happens because of it. The very feeling of happiness only registers as such because you've felt its absence.

The best meals come when you're hungry. Sunshine feels glorious after a week of rain. A warm bed is heaven after a cold, windy day. And beer always tastes best when you're stressed. It's the contrast – the shift from grey to gold – that gives the moment its spark. Happiness isn't a constant. It's a punctuation mark – the firework in the dark sky. Constant happiness wouldn't feel like happiness at all. It would feel like a land of sweeping plains: flat, dry, featureless, dull.

There's nothing better than drawing the curtains, dimming the lights and collapsing on the couch after a long, hard day. But if you stay there for the next three weeks, there comes a time when it starts to feel like depression. Champagne is only special if you've spent a few years drinking cask wine. If your football team won every week, there would come a year when collecting premierships would just lose its thrill and you'd start watching tennis or darts.

Even life's most exquisite pleasures dull without contrast. That dream job? That perfect relationship? That divine croque monsieur from a Parisian boulangerie, with the gruyere that is so magnifique? Given enough time, they all become ... meh. Because uninterrupted bliss doesn't feel amazing. It doesn't feel like anything at all. As American philosopher Noah Lemos said, 'Constant euphoria is the fastest route to indifference.' Pleasant, predictable and slowly driving you nuts, much like a work colleague who likes to use the word 'babe'.

So the idea that we should be happy all the time? Like assembling a fold-out couch from IKEA without giving some thought to killing your spouse, it's not just hard; it's completely impossible. Happiness cannot be a permanent resident in our lives. It can only ever come for a visit. Constant joy and fulfilment wouldn't be joyful and fulfilling. Constant fun wouldn't be fun at all.

And yet, the world keeps telling us sadness is the enemy, that feeling down reflects some kind of problem. That if you're not relentlessly cheerful, then something is wrong with you (but don't worry, HR's got your back, babe).

This book is the story of how this delusion came to be. And why worrying so much about whether or not we are 'happy' is just making us sad.

2

IT'S A HARD-KNOCK LIFE

When life was nasty, brutish and short

For most of history, there was no such thing as the pursuit of happiness. Life's goal was to survive and reproduce.

Yuval Noah Harari, *Sapiens*, 2011

The term 'prehistoric' is thrown around quite a lot these days, generally in reference to my fashion sense or that carton of milk in the back of my fridge. But how many of my critics actually know what the word means? Much like the porn stars Ben Dover and Peter O'Tool, the clue is very much in the name. 'Prehistoric' literally means 'prehistorical records', as in the time before anyone bothered to carve their thoughts into stone or scribble some stick figures onto a parchment. The long, murky era when humans were hunting, gathering, sleeping in caves and trying not to accidentally shag a Neanderthal.

This means that, much like when I try to make small talk at art galleries, everything we say about our prehistoric ancestors is, at best, a bit of a guess. Archaeologists and anthropologists do their best to work out what they ate, where they lived, how they hunted and so on. But when it comes to what they thought, felt and dreamed, much like the moustache's recent return to fashion, these are all mysteries that will never be solved.

All things considered, this makes for a bit of a blind spot. If you were to condense the entire history of Homo sapiens into a single 24-hour day, writing and drawing don't actually kick off until about 11.38pm. (The first pyramids rise at 11.44pm, Rome peaks at 11.58pm and I learned how to parallel park just a squidge before midnight.)

Everything before 11.38pm? Prehistory. A pitch-black void of eternal nothingness. A closed book containing no words.

But since when has knowing nothing ever stopped an academic? I certainly don't see why it should stop me. So ... to business. What did our prehistoric ancestors actually think about happiness?

Well, my guess is they didn't think about it that much. Or indeed, they didn't think much at all. Do you remember the scene in the movie *Cast Away* when a starving, sunburnt and bedraggled Tom Hanks sits down to ponder the point of existence? Or that scene in *The Revenant* when, abandoned in the snow after being mauled by a bear, Leonardo DiCaprio has an existential crisis?

No, you don't. Because these scenes never happened. Nietzsche-style musings on the meaning and purpose of life are a luxury reserved for people who expect life to continue – for example, affluent 21st-century Westerners who buy books with titles like *The Importance of Being Miserable* (or are unfortunate enough to receive one as a gift). Put Tom Hanks in a warm, cosy cafe with a half-caf, oat-milk mocha-latte and *then* he'll start to wonder what life's all about. He'll start to think, 'Sure, I'm successful, but what's it all for?' Life goals are for people who don't have to worry about being bitten by a snake, or dying of frostbite, or getting diarrhoea in an age before pants. Life goals are for people who have four walls, a roof, a fridge full of food, access to penicillin and a workable phone charger.

Did early humans have such luxuries? No, they did not. Even though most people today are rightly worried about climate change, it's worth pointing out that the 21st century is actually something of a golden age when it comes to sustaining life on this planet. For its first two billion years, Earth was a molten hellscape. A collection of swirling, twirling toxic gases, all coming in at 500 degrees Celsius. We're talking about a place that was even more uninhabitable than a Holiday Inn – and for a billion years after that, it wasn't all that much better. Up until about 10,000 years ago, constant ice ages gripped the globe and super volcanoes blocked out the sun. Earthquakes and mega-tsunamis continually tore apart coastlines, and asteroids slammed down without warning. There's a good reason why 99.9 per cent of every species that ever lived is extinct. Planet Earth was basically a barrage of environmental sucker punches, every one of them delivered straight to the nuts.

So yes, by all means, worry about the future. But also be glad that you didn't live in the past. Earth tried very, very hard to kill us – and by and large, it did very well. We humans, after all, used to have heaps of cousins. Earth was once home to not just Neanderthals but also Homo habilis, Homo erectus, Homo floresiensis and the newly discovered Homo naledi. Big-browed, barrel-chested and not short of hair, these guys might have struggled to get a career on the catwalks of Paris and Milan. But they still looked a whole lot like us. And look around and you'll see that they're gone.

We Homo sapiens came very close to joining them. Genetic evidence suggests that around 70,000 years ago, the global population may have dropped to as few as 1200 people, all packed into the southern coast of Africa. One cyclone, one super-flu or severe drought, and that would've been that for humankind. There would have been no art or science. No Mozart or Picasso. James Joyce would never have written *Ulysses*, and none of us would have to pretend that we've read it.

Staying alive, in short, wasn't a walk in the park. It was more like a hike through the desert. A hike undertaken with broken ankles, no feet, a blindfold, bad knees, a nasty cold and some intestinal worms. With sabre-toothed cats just behind you and sudden flash floods up ahead. Every day was an episode of *Alone*, only with fewer snacks and no chance of a Netflix deal.

And if you somehow managed to find a safe cave and remain warm and fed throughout winter, we are talking about a time without antibiotics. A time when the tiniest splinter could kill and infected teeth meant a lifetime of pain. Stubbed toes, dodgy water, uncooked meat – any sort of ailment that might today merit a quick trip to the chemist could back then easily mean a slow death.

But what doesn't kill you must make you stronger, correct? In this mollycoddled age of cars, shops and slankets, many people believe that we modern humans must be inferior specimens. That our ancestors must have been fitter, stronger and healthier than us, thanks to all that exercise, organic food and fresh air.

But it's important to remember that most people are idiots. Far from being super(wo)men, studies in paleodemography suggest the average life expectancy of early humans was around thirty years – and that most kids didn't make it past five.

If you need proof that the good old days were probably bad, look no further than Ötzi the Iceman. A frozen corpse recently found in the Austrian Alps, Ötzi would be about 3350 years old today had he not died in his early 40s. But despite being Europe's best-preserved caveman, this was not a body in the best of health. In among arrow wounds, broken bones and various signs of malnutrition, studies show Ötzi was battling a host of parasitic infections at the time of his death, together with osteoarthritis, atherosclerosis and what appears to have been Lyme disease.

In short, it's hard to believe Ötzi spent his life trying to feel good. He would have been too busy trying to stay on his toes – and not lose those toes to gangrene. One suspects he was less concerned with questions like 'How can I be happy?' and more concerned with questions like 'What the fuck was that noise?' Not to mention, 'Why's my pee turning green?'

Now none of this is to say that prehistoric humans were incapable of feeling pleasure. It's simply to suggest that pleasure came in short bursts. A good day was when you found a dry cave, lit a warm fire and managed to remove some infected pus from your foot.

But I'm not just relying on *The Revenant* here. Biology has some things to say too. Another reason why early humans weren't constantly content is that being constantly content would have got them killed. If workplaces have taught me anything, it's that the survival of the fittest favours the stressed. Evolution rewards the restless – the twitchy, the alert, the neglected, the neurotic, the ones always planning ahead. We live in a world designed for the kind of people who keep us awake during meetings just so they can ask endless questions, then send everyone a fourteen-point email in order to 'follow up'.

According to American biologist Robert Sapolsky, 'We're not built for sustained happiness. We're built for survival.' Like all animals, our brains didn't evolve to feel endless contentment; they evolved to keep us anxiously striving, because anxious striving is what keeps you alive. There may have been Homo sapiens who spent their days smelling the roses. But you and I are more likely to be descended from people who only ever looked at a rose bush to make sure it wasn't hiding a wolf.

Early humans who were naturally laid-back, peaceful and content with their lot weren't hunting mammoths, inventing fire-starting techniques or packing up kids to migrate before the glacier arrived. They weren't constantly scanning the horizon for the next meal, the next idea, the next threat. They would've been the ones who stayed behind. And froze. Or starved. Or got stomped by something with tusks.

Your brain, quite simply, doesn't want you to be content. Yes, it lets you experience happiness, but only in the way an aeroplane offers snacks: briefly satisfying, never quite enough and always accompanied by a gloomy awareness that, elsewhere in the world, other people are eating foie gras.

Back in 1926, American physiologist Walter Cannon coined the term *homeostasis* to describe the human body's endless fussiness. Just like Goldilocks, only slightly less naff, your organs insist on everything being *just right* – not too hot, not too cold and with the perfect balance of salt, sugar, fat, calcium and so on. When anything veers off course, your body jumps into action, tweaking temperature, hormone levels, blood sugar and more in a frantic effort to restore equilibrium.

And this relentless fine-tuning doesn't stop at the neck. The brain is just as obsessive. Serotonin and dopamine – those much-hyped chemicals of pleasure – are tightly rationed. The brain doles out just enough to keep you moving, then slams on the brakes. Without this neurochemical micromanagement, you'd either be paralysed by bliss, like a junkie in a gutter, or stuck on a tear-sodden couch, paralysed by despair.

Take dopamine. Often confused with happiness, it's really just a chemical prod, a restless nudge that says, 'Go on, chase that thing.' But here's the kicker: dopamine is about *wanting*, not *having*. The pursuit excites; the prize quickly disappoints. Your brain resets the pleasure dial every time, ensuring that even when things go well, satisfaction is short-lived. Chocolate, applause, flirtation – they all fade. Even the big stuff – buying a couch, having a baby, parking your car without hearing a crash – comes with a brief high before your brain shrugs and says, 'What's next?'

In short, your brain has a reset button and it's been hitting it since birth. Evolution didn't design you to be content; it designed you to be alert. Because in the grand scheme of things, the moment you feel truly, deeply in love with your life ... is probably the moment you accidentally stroll off a cliff.

3

QUE SERA, SERA

When your fate depended on the moods of the gods

The gods are deaf to our cries and unbending in their wrath.

Homer, *The Iliad*, circa 750 BCE

Having grown up safe and snug in the city, I can't say I know much about farming. Plants and/or animals are definitely involved in some way, though exactly how I have never been certain, and your average farmer also seems to require flannel shirts, gum boots, a shotgun, a ute, right-wing views and a hatred of rabbits. But apart from complaining about droughts and/or complaining about floods, I'm not entirely sure how farmers fill up their days, and there are times when I feel like I should. Farming, after all, has given me the food I eat, the clothes I wear and the topic for the chapter I'm writing.

Ten thousand years ago, however, I wouldn't have felt this way – and that's not just because I hadn't been born yet. It's because at the time, farming hadn't been born either. Stuck in a never-ending series of climate catastrophes, human beings were living like backpackers – hanging out in small groups, constantly on the move, eating, drinking, shagging, scratching but otherwise unemployed.

But then the most recent ice age ended and everything changed – or at least started to – in one part of the world. Probably the biggest game changer in human history (unless you want to count the time we invented the air fryer), the Agricultural Revolution saw a handful of humans discover something extraordinary. Instead of spending all their time running around like headless chooks trying to kill or find food, they decided to grow food and raise chooks for themselves.

And so the age of farming kicked off. Corn, wheat, milk, eggs, barley, rice, beef, lentils, chickpeas, olives, grapes, goats, sheep and pigs: pretty much every single staple of the modern human diet directly dates back to this time. And because our ancestors weren't always wandering from one spot to the next in search of fresh fruit or a stray herd of bison, they were able to put down roots in a metaphorical sense too – that is, settle down in one spot. Much like my own first house, these early structures weren't so great (we're talking mud-brick, thatched-roof, no master bedroom), but on the upside, they generally meant not freezing to death. And, better still, having a chance to store food. For the first time in their 300,000-year history, humans didn't have to eat everything within a few days of plucking it off a bush or spearing it in the neck. They could dry it, pickle it, salt it and ferment it. The ability to grow and store food is the main reason why the tiny handful of humans alive 10,000 years ago has now swelled to a global population of over eight billion.

On a less positive note, all these new-fangled developments eventually led to villages, some of which grew into towns. Equipped with cupboards full of food and a degree of peace, time and comfort, the inhabitants of these places began to work on what we loosely call Western civilisation. And a whole lot of work was required.

Before 10,000 BCE, life had been simple. If you attended to the small matter of staying alive during the day, it was probably cold, dark and time for a nap. But when we stopped moving and started to claim our own land, life started to become a lot more complicated.

For starters, there was the issue of time. When you're hunting, you don't need a schedule – you eat when you can, sleep when it's dark and find shelter when it starts to rain. But farming required knowing when to plant and when to harvest. So, early civilisations started tracking the sun, moon and seasons. The Babylonians were mapping constellations as early as 1200 BCE and the ancient Egyptians aligned their calendar with the annual flooding of the Nile. With this came the concept of calendars, schedules, deadlines and the general stress of feeling 'behind'.

More stressful still was dealing with other people. The birth of agriculture also meant the birth of 'private property', with every would-be farmer suddenly fencing off some dirt and keeping whatever harvest it wrought. 'This is mine' became a thing people said, along with 'get your hands off my sheep'. Inevitably, fights broke out, which someone else had to settle. Governments were soon in business, writing laws, issuing taxes and overseeing public works projects like canals and roads.

But for such laws to be effective, people needed to take notes, which led to the invention of writing. History's first writers weren't poets and philosophers; they were accountants and bureaucrats. Truly ancient literature isn't about love and fate, gods and monsters and man's eternal struggle against man. It's about taxes, debts and lists of supplies. If you like grain storage, you're in for a treat.

Meanwhile, trade took off as well. But the problem with just swapping one thing for another was that the deals could get a touch imprecise. No one wanted to be stuck in a situation where they had to swap an entire pig for a handful of grain, or their favourite spade for a few ears of corn. So, money was duly invented, and inequality came along for the ride. Some people got rich; other people got to work for them; and a few unlucky souls found themselves somebody's slave.

The developing economy also created opportunities for new jobs, such as running a temple on behalf of the gods. Originally confined to the occasional chant around a campfire, religion slowly became a more extensive, organised and all-consuming affair.

And with religion and wealth came war. When your tribe owned next to nothing and was forever on the move, no one cared what they were up to. But when they lived in a town with gold, grain and temples devoted to some demon, they were suddenly worth fighting. Armies grew bigger and spears got sharper as warfare became a full-time job.

And so, what started as a simple idea around 10,000 BCE – 'How about we just plant a few seeds and put up a fence?' – eventually spiralled into the complex shenanigans of modern life. Cities and villages, governments and taxes, status and property, writing and religion, money and war. By 3000 BCE, most Westerners had traded a life of constant wandering for a life of constant wrangling. Western civilisation had begun and there was no turning back.

But what about constant happiness? Now that peace and comfort were easier to come by, had that kicked off too? Well, full disclosure: I wasn't there, so I don't really know. But that said, I think the answer is 'no'.

Life, you see, was still pretty fragile. Disease and starvation remained part of the deal. Sure, people weren't being assaulted by bears as much, but they were developing new and fun ways to feel shit. Slavery and war weren't exactly for everyone, and with large groups of people suddenly living cheek by jowl, diseases and bacteria spread faster than a celebrity nip slip. Archaeological studies of ancient urban centres like Mohenjo-Daro in what's now Pakistan, or Uruk in today's Iraq, have uncovered mass graves and signs of widespread illness. And thanks to the shift to high-carb diets, tooth decay seems to have skyrocketed. Analysis of Egyptian mummies regularly reveals worn-down teeth, infected gums and abscesses the size of a golf ball. It's almost enough to make you glad we have dentists.

On top of that, being reliant on just a few staple crops meant that when those crops failed – thanks to drought, pests, floods or frost – entire communities faced a long, painful diet. Much like nose hair in middle age, famine wasn't an occasional visitor. It was a regular guest.

Happiness, in short, was still hard to come by. If you managed to reach adulthood with all four limbs intact, you could still count yourself pretty lucky.

As we can tell from the few written records that still exist, 'luck' really was the key word. Remember that scene in *The Matrix*, when Keanu Reeves learns that human agency is just an illusion? While we believe we control our own lives, we're actually just the playthings of a mysterious higher power.

Before 500 BCE, most Westerners weren't under any illusions. They knew they were living in a matrix. They knew they had no control. Tell an ancient Egyptian he had the power to shape his own destiny and he would've laughed in your face. He could be the best farmer in Shunet El Zebib, but he knew that any crops he might grow would come from the sun, soil and rain – elements which were all under the control of the gods. If things went well, it was because the gods had decided not to smite him that day. And if a crop failed, then clearly they had.

Today, God is by and large a benevolent figure – supportive, patient, always available for a chat (so long as you don't expect him to say something back). Sort of like a life coach, only less likely to post shit on LinkedIn, he's the kind of god who wants you to follow your dreams, eat all your vitamins and remember that 'everything happens for a reason'.

Back then, however, gods were more like celestial scriptwriters. Temperamental, petty and unfeeling creatives who saw us as nothing more than characters in a show – and not a nice, gentle BBC period drama, either. We're talking about a gruesome, blood-splattered horror film, or at the very least, *Game of Thrones*. Ancient gods were gods who got bored easily and treated tragedy like a narrative twist. Because struggle, of course, is the essence of storytelling. Who wants to see a show where everything starts out well, continues to go well and then ends with everything being tickety-boo? Certainly not Zeus or Thor. If something good happened –a bountiful harvest or a healthy child – it wasn't because you deserved it. It was because the plot demanded it.

Even in a time of ceramics and cosmetics and chariots and cheese, a time of unprecedented progress and wealth, the average person still didn't see happiness as something they were able to pursue, let alone something they could begin to expect. Life was just about getting through the day and hoping the gods didn't decide to smite you. Enjoyment wasn't the result of hard work, a good attitude or strategic choices; it was a freak event. A rare and fleeting gift from the gods, bestowed on a lucky few.

Happiness, in short, was something that happened – or didn't. It came uninvited, like the weather, and it was just as unpredictable. If you want proof of how deeply this idea runs through ancient thinking, look at the language we still use today. Nearly every European word for 'happiness' traces back to the word *luck*. The Old Norse root *hap* meant *chance* or *fortune* and it still lingers in words like *happenstance* (a lucky occurrence), *perhaps* (if luck allows) and *mishap* (a small misfortune).

Other languages echo the same worldview. In German, *Glück* means both *luck* and *happiness*. The French *heureux* comes from *heur*, meaning *chance*. In ancient Greek, *eutychia* combines *eu-* (good) and *tychē* (luck, or the goddess of fortune). And in the Romance languages – *felicidade* (Portuguese), *felicidad* (Spanish) and *felicità* (Italian) – all descend from the Latin *felix*, which means *fortunate* or *blessed by fate*.

In other words, for most of history, happiness wasn't a goal. It was a gift.

So how do we know all this guff about the gods? Because the age of literature has finally arrived. Until around 2100 BCE, as far as archaeology can tell, writing was basically a series of spreadsheets. Clay tablets were filled with trades, taxes and tallies. Myths and legends presumably existed, but they were strictly oral.

But in and around what we now call the Middle East, some storytellers started to write their stuff down. Suddenly, we get talking snakes, burning bushes, miraculous births, lion-slaying heroes, dragons hoarding treasure, trees that grant immortality and world-ending floods. Plus, of course, nature gods. So many nature gods. Sky gods hurling lightning. Sea gods drowning sailors. Forest gods making fires. Sun gods craving blood.

And while ancient fiction was, well, fiction, it's worth remembering that at the time it was 'fact'. As Tom Holland (the historian, not the Spider-Man) puts it, 'The ancient mind didn't divide the world into natural and supernatural. The divine was just part of reality.' Storytelling wasn't about passing time; it was about making sense of the world. A world that, quite clearly, didn't care about us. A world that just did what it did – randomly, brutally and often at the worst possible moment.

So they gave that random brutality a face. Well, okay, several faces. The gods were the first great explanatory system. Every natural force got a name, a backstory and some kind of serious personality disorder. Rain was a sky god sobbing uncontrollably. Earthquakes were someone having a tantrum beneath your feet. Thunder was a divine war hammer slamming into the heavens. The wind was a god whispering a threat through the trees.

Just like nature, these gods didn't particularly like us. At best, they tolerated us like background noise. At worst, they actively resented us. These were gods of blood, fire, war and vengeance. The kind who wiped out entire cities by means of flood, fire, famine and plague. Gods who demanded animal sacrifices, human sacrifices, virgin sacrifices – anything that could bleed – and even then might still smite for fun. They weren't protectors or mentors; they were divine toddlers with unlimited power and no emotional regulation. You didn't worship them out of love. You worshipped them because you didn't want your crops to rot or to wake up with some strange growth on your penis.

But in a strange way, they helped the world make sense. Why did your boat sink? A sea god was grumpy. Why did you miscarry? A fertility god was testing you. Or punishing you. Or just having a bad day. Religion was born out of fear, but it gave that fear a script. Cosmic indifference got dressed up as the will of the gods. And these gods didn't care about happiness.

Let's begin by looking at the world's oldest story, *The Epic of*

Gilgamesh. Composed on clay tablets around 2100 BCE and set in a land we now call Iraq, it's the world's oldest argument that happiness isn't something you earn – it's something the gods might or might not give you for kicks.

King Gilgamesh, you see, has almost everything: strength, power, a magnificent beard and craven subjects who cower before him. But despite all these divine blessings, he's still not happy. All that violence, glory and bloodshed haven't managed to fill the void.

So the gods send him Enkidu, a wild man of the steppe, to be his new best friend. Possibly bonding over their terrible names, the two go on various sadistic adventures. They slay monsters. Rape newlyweds. Force innocent young men into slavery. And finally, for a while, Gilgamesh is happy. Not because he has conquered something, but because he has connected with someone.

Then, plot twist! Enkidu dies. The gods have killed him off with a sudden illness, because ... well, just because it's Act 2. Gilgamesh is devastated, heartbroken and suddenly obsessed with his own mortality. 'Must I die too? Must I be as lifeless as Enkidu? Grief has entered into my heart. I am afraid of death.'

So begins a desperate, doomed quest for eternal life – a spiritual crisis that predates *Eat Pray Love* by about 4000 years but somehow manages to feel more relevant. Gilgamesh journeys to the edge of the world and wrestles with the meaning of existence. But ultimately, he fails to find either happiness or immortality. Not because he wasn't strong or brave or clever, but because he's human – and humans don't get to decide.

By the end, Gilgamesh finally gets it. Even for the mightiest king on Earth, happiness isn't something you can chase or secure.

It's fleeting, fragile and entirely beyond our control. The gods giveth and the gods taketh away. But generally speaking, they prefer to taketh.

Another way to phrase this might be 'man is clay and straw and the god is his builder', but I wouldn't want to plagiarise *The Maxims of Ani*, even though Ani's probably too dead to sue. A collection of life lessons written on papyrus way back in 1300 BCE, this Egyptian self-help book might not be considered helpful by the sort of people who read such things today. There are no morning routines, no mantras and no manifestation techniques, just a big dose of fatalism, delivered in tones of despair.

Don't bother working hard, Ani advises, or at least don't expect anything good to result from it. Life is cruel and 'no man may rise by his own efforts'. Success, if it comes at all, is temporary, and for all you know it could be a trap. 'Do not boast of your wealth,' he also advises. 'It is not yours forever.' And if you're hoping that finding true love might at least be worthwhile, this gloomy Gus would like a short word. 'Do not place your heart in the hand of a woman.' And if that hasn't cheered you up, don't forget you could die at any second. 'Man knows not the span of his days; God alone determines the length of his life.'

To Ani's readers – that is, his fellow Egyptians –this probably just seemed like common sense. After all, they lived in a world teeming with gods who had crocodile heads, demon fangs, obsidian knives and fire-spitting cobras perched on their helmets. Divine stability wasn't exactly a strong suit.

And no deity illustrated this more than Hathor. Tasked with a wide-ranging portfolio, this ancient Egyptian goddess was in charge of joy, love, music and pleasure, and the divine patron of celebration and dance. If she smiled upon you, life was good: wine flowed, music played, friends gathered and love bloomed.

But if Hathor was in a bad mood? Tough luck. No amount of effort, prayer or positive thinking could cheer her up. Happiness under her reign wasn't a reward – it was a privilege and a fleeting one at that. One day, she might adore you; the next, she might kill you. In some myths, she transforms into Sekhmet, the lion-headed goddess of vengeance and slaughter. A god who once got so drunk on blood she nearly wiped out humanity. Same goddess, different vibe. A divine Jekyll and Hyde.

For the Egyptians, happiness was a passing whim of the gods, not the outcome of self-discipline or self-knowledge. It came when they allowed it and vanished when they didn't, which is quite a long way from 'choose joy'.

The ancient Greeks were equally upbeat. 'Call no man happy until he is dead,' Herodotus cheerfully advised his compatriots, because as long as you were alive, fate could still turn against you. You might think you're doing fine – wealth, friends, family, goat herd in order – but then, bang: plague, war, goat stampede.

In Greek mythology, the world wasn't fair – and neither were the gods. That was the point. Living in golden, incestuous luxury atop Mount Olympus, these weren't benevolent sky-dwellers handing out blessings. They were spiteful, jealous, childish and vengeful – the kind of deities who started plagues, wars and fires just for fun. Zeus, for example, was a serial rapist, while Poseidon drowned sailors just because it was Wednesday. Apollo once killed a group of kids because someone insulted his mum, while Artemis had a man ripped apart by his own dogs because he accidentally saw her naked. Athena turned a woman into a spider, while Dionysus – in perhaps the most unforgivable crime of them all – once got drunk and invented theatre.

The point here is that justice wasn't the point. The gods played favourites, settled personal scores and generally behaved like (a slim and tanned) Donald Trump. You could be thriving one day and doomed the next, just because that was how the dice fell. The Trojan War, for example, wasn't started by the citizens of Troy – they were just the folks who got killed. According to Homer, the (possibly mythical) poet from around 750 BCE, this catastrophic, decade-long bloodbath began because a bunch of goddesses started to bicker about which one was the hottest. So they forced a Trojan prince to pick. He chose Aphrodite, thereby pissing off the others and prompting them to cause a war as revenge.

On a similar note, Achilles – the greatest Greek warrior of the day and central character in Homer's *Iliad* – chooses to fight in Troy not because he cares about the cause or expects to survive. He fights and dies because he knows that to fight and die is his destiny. 'Fate is the same for the man who holds back, the same if he fights hard. We are all held in the same fate, whether we sit still or run into battle.'

Even the greatest warrior in the world cannot hope to win a fight on his own. His victories will only ever be temporary. His fate will always be sealed. Good or bad, the outcome is already decided because Zeus and co get to call all the shots. In other words: don't bother trying to find happiness. Just hope the gods are in a good mood.

After Greece came Rome, a small city-state in central Italy that slowly grew into a continent-spanning colossus. Engineers, soldiers and slave-owners, they conquered everything from Britain to Babylon in the course of building the greatest empire the world had ever seen.

But while their military tactics were uniquely Roman, their gods were mostly borrowed. Zeus became Jupiter, Ares became Mars, Dionysus became Bacchus and Poseidon was rebranded as Neptune. And like their Greek originals, the Roman gods weren't exactly moral role models. They were dysfunctional narcissists who liked to liven things up. They didn't reward virtue or punish vice. They reminded you, more or less every day, that the universe was not designed with your feelings in mind.

But the Romans did come up with at least one noteworthy god of their own. For all their discipline and self-belief, they knew that life could turn on a dime. Fortune frequently favoured the brave, but it could also favour cowardly schmucks. So naturally, they invented a goddess for that too: Fortuna, the goddess of luck.

Capricious, cruel and deeply disloyal, Fortuna was worshipped by emperors, generals and commoners alike. Soldiers sacrificed to her before battles. Politicians begged for her favour before elections. And when things inevitably fell apart – wars, plagues, failed harvests – Romans didn't go to therapy. They blamed Fortuna and her famously foul mood. One day, she'd cover you in glory; the next, she'd throw you off a cliff. As Publilius Syrus famously wrote, 'Fortune is like glass: when it shines brightest, it shatters.' The moment when everything is going really well is generally the moment when it all goes to shit.

Obsessed with gambling and always on the lookout for omens, the Roman worldview was brutally simple: life is chaos, luck is everything and fate always wins in the end. You might be destined for triumphs, statues and coins with your face on them – or a messy death in the arena. Either way, there's not much point in worrying. Picture life as a chariot with no steering wheel, dodgy brakes and a drunk god at the reins. Your job as a Roman was to hold on for as long as Fortuna would let you.

But what about the Bible? And by that, I mean the Old Testament, that slightly bizarre collection of stories dating back to around 600 BCE. A lot happens in this book, quite apart from the bit where God creates the entire universe. There's rampant incest, severed foreskins, talking donkeys and a woman who's made out of salt. My favourite scene sees forty-two children get mauled by a bear because they told the prophet Elisha that he was going a bit bald.

Not a lot makes sense in these pages, but there's at least one point on which they are crystal clear. 'The God of all gods and Lord of all lords' can get a touch cranky at times. While not, perhaps, quite as bad as my ex, this is a god who rains down fire on cities, drowns the world in a flood, turns rivers to blood and kills babies just to help make a point. And just like my ex, when He's in one of His moods, there's really nothing much you can do. In Ecclesiastes, King Solomon said, 'The race is not to the swift, nor the battle to the strong, nor bread to the wise, nor riches to men of understanding, nor favour to men of skill; but time and chance happeneth to them all.'

While God occasionally rewards the righteous and punishes the wicked, there are plenty of times when He does just the opposite, based on nothing more than a whim. The Old Testament is filled with innocent, blameless, seemingly praiseworthy people who suddenly find themselves in deep shit.

Take Job (from, well, The Book of Job). He's a good man. He's righteous, devout, 'blameless and upright'. The kind of guy you'd trust to look after your favourite camel, or at least one of your kids. Then, just like that, his entire life is obliterated. His wealth? Gone. His health? Wrecked. His children? All dead in a storm. The reason? God has made a bet with Satan. 'Sure, Job worships you now,' the Lord of Darkness had said, 'but ruin his life and then see what happens.' And God goes, 'Okay, champ, you're on.'

Or take Noah and his ark. He happens to live in a time when the world is corrupt and God has decided that the only measured and responsible course is to kill almost all living things. By sheer luck, Noah is the only man to get a leave pass. While the rest of humanity drowns, he and his family get to float in a zoo. There's no mention of Noah being especially deserving; he's not feeding the poor or rescuing kittens or helping old ladies to cross the street. He just happens to be the guy that God picked.

And if the Lord's favour is unpredictable, so is His wrath. God, we're told, is 'a jealous God', 'an avenging God', a consuming fire who 'takes vengeance and is filled with wrath'. In the Old Testament, entire cities are wiped off the map, along with all of their inhabitants. Sodom and Gomorrah are destroyed with fire and brimstone; Jericho is flattened with the blow of a trumpet; the Amalekites are wiped out, down to their last sheep. Even God's chosen people, the Israelites, spent centuries as slaves before being 'rescued' via ten plagues that included darkness, frogs, boils, locusts and death. And despite being so busy with all this smiting, God also finds time to create leprosy, scatter snakes here and there, and saddle the Philistines with a bad case of haemorrhoids.

In short, for most of ancient history, your life was in the lap of the gods. Good deeds wouldn't take you far. If the gods were on your side, you'd prosper. If they weren't, you wouldn't. And good luck trying to understand why. Much like getting planning permission from my local council, happiness was just something that either happened or that didn't. A mysterious stroke of luck entirely beyond your control. Not a thing to understand or pursue.

4

THE POWER

When your fate started depending on you

Happiness depends upon ourselves.
Aristotle, *Nicomachean Ethics*, circa 350 BCE

Much like family gatherings, history can sometimes get a bit messy. Events that ought to be neatly tucked away in one particular timeline can sometimes spill out into others or, worse, pop up somewhere else. Did you know, for example, that Oxford University (founded in 1096) is quite a bit older than the Aztec Empire (founded in 1428)? Or that Cleopatra lived closer in time to the Moon landing than she did to the people who built Egypt's big pyramids?

But neat freaks need not despair, because sometimes a tidy little box can appear out of nowhere. It turns out some of history's biggest names were alive at the same time, living very different lives side by side. Leonardo da Vinci and Niccolò Machiavelli both had the same boss. Abraham Lincoln and Charles Darwin were both born on the same day in 1805. And the very same year Columbus was 'discovering' America, Michelangelo was busy sculpting the statue of David and Copernicus was proving that the Earth orbits the sun.

Which brings us to the fifth century BCE – a little slice of time that, seemingly out of nowhere, gave us some of the world's biggest brains. It was as if someone had found a genius tap and let it run and run.

You want names? Well, good news, I have some. And 'Confucius' is the first on the list. Over in China, he was laying down a blueprint for social harmony that continues to shape Eastern thought to this day. Confucius didn't just influence philosophy; he influenced everything from government exams to dinner table etiquette.

Over in what's now Nepal, a certain Prince Siddhartha Gautama found himself having a full-blown existential crisis of the sort only a prince could afford. Unable to shake constant thoughts about pain and suffering (even though he lived in an age before people started to say 'yeet', 'bruh' and 'rizz'), he snuck out of his palace one summer's day to spend a month or so sitting under a tree. When he got up, it was because he'd been struck by some insights. In said moment, Prince Siddhartha became 'the awakened one'. Or, as he's better known, 'the Buddha'.

In India, the early texts of what would become modern Hinduism – the Upanishads and Vedas – were being written, while over in Iran, a guy with the usual name of Zoroaster came up with the concept of cosmic dualism: a universe governed by an eternal struggle between evil and good. 'Christian' concepts like heaven, hell, Satan and angels all owe a lot to his work.

And Zoroaster's influence was almost certainly felt in the rugged hill country of Canaan, the home of a small group of tribes mostly known as the Hebrews. Some of their scribes went on to produce what we now call the Old Testament, a scattered collection of texts that introduced a single, radical idea: instead of a divine pantheon of feuding nutbags, there was just one supreme, invisible, all-powerful God who, it turned out, was not to be trifled with.

Further west, a group of long-bearded toga-wearers were starting to have a few thoughts of their own. Tired of building ships and eating dips, ancient Greek philosophers like Pythagoras, Heraclitus,

Anaximander and Thales of Miletus suddenly took it upon themselves to ask the big questions: 'What is truth?', 'What is reality?' and 'And what is the point of existence?'

Hot on their sandalled heels came plenty more 'lovers' of 'wisdom' – or, as the Greeks phrased it, *philos* of *sophia*. But Socrates, Plato, Aristotle and the gang weren't just philosophers; they were civilisational architects: men who, between them, laid the groundwork for science, logic, ethics, politics, mathematics, democracy, biology, epistemology, critical thinking and moral philosophy. Pretty much every time you've ever had an original thought, you can be sure one of them had it first.

China, Nepal, India, Greece, Iran, Israel. So many different places. So many different thinkers. All around the same time. Is this just a lucky roll of the historical dice, another weird historical coincidence, like John F Kennedy, CS Lewis and Aldous Huxley all dying on the same day?

Well, you *could* say that, I suppose. But if you did, I would say you're wrong. Zoom out a touch and you'll see the historical dice were all loaded. All these different parts of the world weren't all that different.

In 1943, the psychologist Abraham Maslow – a man responsible for the phrase 'Maslow's Hierarchy of Needs' (and, no doubt, many deeply dull dinner parties) – famously argued that humans have ... well ... a hierarchy of needs. That if we don't have enough food, water, shelter and safety, such things tend to be our sole focus. But once those basic needs are met, we can stop worrying about dying and start worrying about living. Bigger, messier questions emerge. What's the point of all this? What makes life meaningful? Why do I feel vaguely hollow inside?

And that's where history kicks in. By around 500 BCE, humans had been farming for roughly 9000 years, which meant we had more or less got the hang of it. In the age-old battle against the forces of nature, Homo sapiens were finally notching up a few wins. If a farmer's crops failed or he lost a few sheep, he might still blame fate or the wrath of the gods, but deep down, he probably knew he'd stuffed up. That with a sturdier grain silo and fewer holes in the fence, things might have turned out differently.

And it wasn't just farmers. All over the world, people were beginning to realise they weren't entirely at the mercy of droughts and floods, locusts and wolves, bandits or marauding barbarians. Roads were being paved. Laws were being standardised. Houses were warm (or at least warmer than caves). Food surpluses were common. Trade was thriving. Cities were flourishing. Empires were stable. People were – at least by prehistoric standards – living pretty well.

And, best of all, they had time. Time to sit. Time to talk. Time to think. For the first time in history, large numbers of people didn't have to spend twenty-plus hours a day labouring in a field, tracking a buffalo or protecting their kill from wild dogs. They had roofs over their heads, granaries full of wheat and fresh water not too far away. And with their basic needs taken care of, their brains began to drift elsewhere.

It was a time German-Swiss philosopher Karl Jaspers would later call the 'Axial Age' – a time 'when man became conscious of Being as a whole, of himself and his limitations'. And, in the process, developed a fondness for monologues.

So maybe it wasn't a cosmic coincidence that Aristotle, Buddha and Confucius all lived around the same time. They were, in a sense, the world's first Arts students – the long-haired kind who live at home, smoke too much dope, bang on about politics and start a crap podcast. These weren't people who had to think about hunting or harvesting. They were people who could think for the sake of thinking itself. And think about the fact that they were thinking.

But, for the purpose of this book, the key point is this: every ancient philosopher had something in common, and I don't just mean deeply bored wives. For most of history, people believed life was dictated by fate, the gods or some cruel, unpredictable cosmic force. Whether you were happy or miserable, rich or poor, healthy or diseased, these were things you couldn't control.

The men who laid the foundations for pretty much all modern thought were the first to dispute this. The first to point out that we might not just be puppets dangling from a string, but independent beings with power and agency. Beings who, through reason, reflection and discipline, might be able to shape our own fate and carve out a 'good life'. As Yuval Noah writes, 'The big philosophical breakthrough of the *Axial Age* was the discovery that humans can aim to completely transcend their worldly condition and the entire natural order.'

And it was a discovery that reverberates to this day. For the first time, people began to imagine that a good life might not just be a matter of luck or divine whim but something a person could actually achieve for themselves. That a good life isn't something handed down from above but something we can craft from within. They were laying down the intellectual foundations of something radical: the idea that human beings – all of us – can take responsibility for our own lives.

It was one of the biggest mindset shifts in history. Before this, the best advice you could give someone was 'hope the gods are in a good mood'. After this, the message became far more powerful: 'Work on yourself. Build good habits. Live well. And maybe, just maybe, make the world a little less awful.' In short, humans were no longer feeling like extras in a show. They were starting to write their own script.

5

ONLY HAPPY WHEN IT RAINS

When Buddha and Confucius became the first killjoys

Happiness does not consist in pastimes and
amusements, but in virtuous activities.
Aristotle, *Nicomachean Ethics*, circa 335 BCE

Have you ever noticed that some people choose to spend their time in ways that are a teensy bit weird? I'm not talking about guys who try to brew their own beer, women who host gender reveal parties or people who watch an entire cricket match from beginning to end. These activities apparently fall into the category of 'stuff that some people find fun'. It takes all types to make a world, even if I often wish that it didn't.

I'm also not talking about activities that are a means to an end. We've all had jobs we hated because of a salary we liked, or taken some horrible medicine to calm our stomach. And who hasn't stayed in a miserable relationship for years on end because it seemed preferable to having that talk?

No, I'm talking about people who don't seem to pursue happiness *at all*. About people who say 'I shouldn't' more than five times a day and are riddled with guilt if they fail to finish a novel. People who read every email, never skip the gym and will always eat the last Brussels sprout. Life for such people is a grim and tedious series of duties. Every day must include a measure of pain.

Historically speaking, it's tempting to describe these people as modern-day Puritans. The least fun thing to come out of Europe since 'the Great Pox' (aka 'syphilis'), the Puritans were a sect of 16th-century

Protestants who liked to burn witches, wear itchy black clothes and give their kids names like 'Despair' and 'Lament'. Haunted by the possibility that someone, somewhere, might somehow be happy, they also set out to strip Christianity of anything remotely pleasant or fun. Plays were pagan, dancing was sinful, Christmas a dangerous cult. Festivals, music, church decorations, alcohol, gambling, sex – all became pit stops on the very short road that led sinners to hell.

But for the real starting point of modern-day misery-seeking, we probably need to return to the Axial Age. Remember when we were back in Chapter 4? After about 300,000 years of hunting and gathering and a few more running terrible farms, humans were finally masters of nature. We'd domesticated animals, planted crops, built cities and mostly stopped being eaten by bears. For the first time in history, we weren't just reacting to the world. We were shaping it.

Which left only one question: what shape did we want? When we ask that question today, we usually mean, 'How do I create a life that feels good?' We want to know what will bring us fulfilment and pleasure.

But things back then were a bit different (and I'm not just referring to the fact that deodorant wasn't a thing). Most ancient ideas of a 'good life' would strike us as pretty bad, because feeling good wasn't one of them. For most philosophers, religious leaders and political figures, emotions we now associate with happiness – joy, pleasure, contentment – weren't just unimportant; they were actively suspicious. If you were having too much fun, you were doing life wrong.

Confucius, for example, was a major-league downer. The kind of guy who'd interrupt a birthday party to lecture kids about the dangers of sugar, then insist on winning Blind Man's Bluff just to teach them a lesson.

Born in 551 BCE in Shandong Province, 'the Sage of Ten Thousand Generations' spent much of his life wandering around what's now called China, politely hectoring people about propriety, ritual and respect. His central message was simple: society works best when everyone knows their place and behaves accordingly. Forget 'living your truth' – your job was to live your role: 'Let the ruler be a ruler, the subject a subject, the father a father, the son a son.' Everyone had a part to play in a pre-written script, and woe betide anyone who wanted to improvise.

For Confucius, the good life was not about chasing happiness. Joy just wasn't the goal. 'He who aims to be happy in all things,' he warned, 'will not escape destruction.' In other words: if you find yourself having too much fun, something's gone wrong. Prepare for disaster. Confucius believed that personal fulfilment came through duty – doing your chores, keeping your word and never questioning your elders. Real virtue was earned through the slow, tedious grind of becoming a decent, respectable human being.

Buddha was also a bit of a buzzkill, despite some warm and fuzzy misconceptions that persist to this day. That fat, jolly statue you see in restaurants? He's not actually the Buddha at all. He's Budai, a Chinese monk who laughed a lot, liked a snack and lived a few centuries later. The real Buddha looked nothing like that. And he had quite a different vibe.

Born a prince in the 5th century BCE, Siddhartha Gautama came into the world swaddled in silk and fed with a silver spoon. Raised in a marble palace, his life was an endless carousel of massages, banquets, dancers and footstools. His father kept him locked away from all signs of sickness, aging or death – an early case of helicopter parenting.

But was this enough to shield him from misery? No, of course not.

As the B-man himself later put it, 'Birth is suffering, aging is suffering, illness is suffering, death is suffering; union with what is displeasing is suffering; separation from what is pleasing is suffering; not to get what one wants is suffering.'

Life, in short, is one big turd. Pleasure is fleeting. Success is an illusion. Comfort is temporary at best. But in our hearts, most of us know this already (particularly if we have teenagers). The prince's big revelation – the one that made him 'the Buddha' – was that wanting life to get better only makes it worse. 'The root of suffering,' he declared, 'is attachment.'

The Buddha's solution, therefore, was to not desire anything (least of all something like 'happiness'). Just detach, he suggested. Sit back and let go. Don't chase satisfaction. Don't cling to outcomes. Don't build your hopes. Stop trying (or worse, expecting) to be happy and – maybe – you'll stop being so sad. Because the less you care, the less life can hurt you.

On the surface, this all sounds rather empowering, but drill down and it's a tad grim. 'Conquering yourself' basically meant giving up not just your desire for pleasure but your desire for anything, including, say, a comfy mattress. Or even a doona and sheet. Buddha, in all likelihood, would not support my secret desire to start playing Dungeons and Dragons. Not because it's deeply uncool, but because trying to have fun is both futile and dangerous.

What about Hinduism? Well, for starters, it's not a single religion in the conventional sense. It's more like a thick stew of gods, philosophies, rituals, poems, chants, sages, yogis, gurus and mystics. A spiritual feast that's been simmering for over 3000 years (and added a lot of key ingredients in 500 BCE).

But when it comes to happiness, the Hindu recipe is fairly consistent. Yes, you can experience pleasure. Worldly joys like success, status, sex, comfort and so forth are all very tasty nibbles ... but please don't for one moment pretend they're a meal. All worldly joy is *maya* – illusion. A shimmering mirage that will not nourish. True happiness isn't something you can whip up with the right ingredients. The goal is to get out of the kitchen altogether, because real happiness is *moksha*: freedom from hunger. Liberation from the eternal cycle of birth, death and rebirth. You find it by putting down your spoon and realising your *atman* (individual self) is already one with Brahman (ultimate reality). Or something like that. Personally, I find it all quite hard to swallow.

As for the world's first major religion, Zoroastrianism, it's the spiritual equivalent of a once-great rock band that basically invented a genre but now doesn't get much airtime. Good and evil? Heaven and hell? Final judgement? Angels and demons? These are all early Zoroastrian hits. And yet the credit usually goes to Judaism, Christianity and Islam – the louder acts that showed up much later.

But not every track was a chart-topper. Unlike many religions that treated joy with deep suspicion, Zoroastrianism saw happiness as a moral duty. 'Happiness comes to the one who brings happiness to others' is a key message of one of the Gathas – the religion's oldest hymns. Holiness wasn't about enduring life nobly until paradise arrived. It was about living well now.

Then along came Alexander the Great, the all-conquering boy king of Macedonia and by all accounts a bit of a hunk. Fond of crushing his enemies, when he wasn't busy brushing his long, golden hair, Alex conquered Persia, torched most of its temples and killed not a few of its priests. Out went Zoroastrianism, together with its weird idea that life was something to enjoyed.

Happiness was off the playlist. And it would be many years before it found its way back.

6

WEST SIDE STORY

How Western thinkers turned suffering into a virtue

Western civilization begins with Greece.
EH Warmington, *Greek Geography*, 1934

But enough about the Eastern overthinkers. This is supposed to be a book about the West. So what, exactly, was going on in these parts, vis-à-vis thoughts about happiness? Well ... not a whole lot, as far as we can tell.

In 500 BCE, the economic machinery that powered the Axial Age – cities, writing, slavery, surplus grain – hadn't yet made it to Australia, North America or most of Europe. By and large, these were still hunter-gatherer cultures, living close to the land and even closer to the edge of survival. And in the absence of clay tablets or scrolls scrawled with 'What is the good life?', it's safe to assume they weren't workshopping grand ethical theories. The big question was less likely to be 'What is happiness?' so much as 'Where the hell can I find some fresh water?'

In Australia, for example, the climate could be punishing. Droughts were long, fires tore through the bush and food sources could vanish with a change in the wind. In more positive news, Kyle Sandilands had not yet been born, but life could still get pretty tough.

In North America, Indigenous nations contended with freezing winters, roaming bison, hostile neighbours and the occasional famine. You weren't sitting under a tree pondering metaphysics when a cougar might pounce at any fucking moment, or an icy storm seemed to be on the way.

And in the dark, muddy forests of Europe, things weren't exactly serene. People lived in small tribal groups, surrounded by wolves, wild boars, rain that never stopped and neighbours who would raid your village for fun. Winters were long, food had to be hoarded and marriage choices were generally limited to your favourite second cousin (i.e. the one without the boils and red rash).

In short, before abstract concepts like 'happiness' could take root, there had to be some margin for abstraction. And in these corners of the world, life hadn't yet made room for armchair philosophy. It was still very much a standing, spear-in-hand kind of existence.

~

Well, that's my theory, anyway. And what we now know about ancient Western gods by and large backs it up. Much like the ancient gods of the east, they were overwhelmingly nature gods – powerful, unpredictable forces you needed to placate at all costs. These weren't deities handing out blessings. They were handing out thunder and blood.

In Australia, for example, the Dreaming tells of the Rainbow Serpent, a sacred creator being who carved out the rivers and mountains, but who could just as easily drown an entire community, should the mood happen to strike. Then there's Tiddalik, the greedy frog who drank all the water on the continent, triggering a long and brutal drought. Such stories aren't just about animals behaving badly. They are warnings about imbalance. For ancient Indigenous cultures, the land was – and remains – a living, breathing, sacred thing. Something to listen to, work with and learn from. It's a worldview that leaves far less room for human arrogance; far less room to get carried away with our power and brainy magnificence.

Ancient Native American stories reflect a similar logic: nature isn't to be mastered but respected and feared. The Wendigo, for example, embodied winter, famine and cannibalism: a grotesque cautionary tale about what happens when humans take more than they need. Then there's Coyote, the wily trickster of countless tribes, who might save the world one day and wreck it the next. These stories firmly placed humans *within* the ecosystem, rather than some realm above it. In these tales, nature always has the final word – and anyone who forgets that usually ends up dead, cursed or transformed into something unpleasant.

Meanwhile, the gods of northwestern Europe weren't all that much more accommodating. The Viking gods, for example, were violent lunatics, the lot of them – think MAGA but with better hats. Odin gouged out his own eye and hanged himself from a tree, while Thor strutted about smashing mountains. Loki, god of mischief, was a full-blown pants man whose offspring included a death-wolf, a giant serpent and a half-rotted underworld goddess. And when the world ends at Ragnarök, we see wolves devouring the sun, gods dying in a bloodbath and the sky being ripped apart in a brawl. These deities *were* nature at its most brutal.

The Celtic gods, for their part, could be more MAGA still. There was Morrígan, the goddess of fate, who showed up at battlefields to snack on the corpses. And Dagda, the giant with a club so massive that one end could kill instantly and the other could bring you back. Much like Donald Trump himself, these gods were loud, shameless and slightly demented reminders that the world could be senseless and cruel.

Unless, of course, you lived in Greece. Or some of its city-states.

Close enough to borrow ideas from Egypt, Babylon and Persia – but isolated enough to mix and match – cities like Athens and Thebes were blessed with geography, trade, time and temperature: the four golden ingredients for an intellectual revolution.

The warm Mediterranean climate meant fewer hours battling wolves, mud or starvation, while fertile land meant reliable harvests. Trade routes brought parchments and scrolls. And best of all – but not in a strict moral sense – Greece had an abundance of slaves. The fact that manual labour was outsourced gave the upper classes 'quiet time for reflection and learning' or, as they termed it, *skholē*. Nowhere did this take root more deeply than in Athens, where free time was practically a civic virtue. While most of Europe was still focused on livestock, weather gods and not marrying their cousins, the Athenians were creating schools, holding symposiums, building libraries and founding temples to logic.

These symposiums were wine-fuelled think-a-thons where bearded men in togas debated justice, reality, government, virtue and whether a chair was a chair or just a 'chairness'. From all this chin-stroking came the foundations of Western thought: democracy, ethics, metaphysics, political theory, natural philosophy and the Socratic method: the ancient Greek tradition of asking so many annoying questions that someone either changes their mind or walks off in a huff. (It's no coincidence that Socrates is the patron saint of insufferable first-year philosophy students. Ugly, barefoot and loathed by his wife, he spent his days harassing strangers with questions like 'What is justice?' and 'Are you *sure* you exist?' until the city authorities finally sentenced him to death.)

So when people call Greece 'the cradle of Western civilisation', they're not just being poetic. They're pointing to a historical fluke. In one sunny, olive-scented corner of the Mediterranean, enough wealthy men had enough free time to philosophise – and, instead of telling them to shut up, other people took notes.

In short, Athens gave us a strange and enduring idea: that it's not only possible, but important, to spend large chunks of your life thinking about what life is for. But for the Athenians, it wasn't for happiness. Take Zeno, for example, a merchant from Cyprus who worked hard his whole life only to lose everything in a shipwreck. Instead of doing what any reasonable person might do – i.e. develop a drinking problem – he decided to spend the rest of his days standing on a painted porch (or *Stoa Poikile*) in the middle of Athens, telling passers-by that feeling good was for suckers.

Eventually gathering a number of followers (this being an age before anti-depressants), Zeno's 'Stoics' took one look at the highs and lows of human existence and decided to give them a miss. Not unlike the Buddha 6000 kilometres further east, their core belief was that external things – money, fame, relationships, success, even your own health – were all more or less none of your business. To the Stoics, life wasn't about pleasure, meaning, friends or family, because all of those things were ultimately subject to fate. If you built your life around them, you were basically due for a fall.

Instead, the only thing that truly mattered was one thing you could control: how you responded to life's endless miseries. If everything they loved was taken away overnight, a true Stoic would not shed a tear. If their house burned down to the ground, along with their wife, kids and dog, they'd simply give a solemn nod and embrace the opportunity to test their self-discipline.

But what doesn't go down also doesn't go up. If a true Stoic never cried or complained, they didn't laugh or celebrate either. Emotional repression was turned into a lifestyle. Joy, grief, anger and excitement were all things to be neutralised by inner strength. Getting married? Maintain your composure. Windfall inheritance? Look stern and move on. A Stoic was expected to treat a cancerous lump and a birthday cake with roughly the same amount of pep in their step. If you took Zeno to a Roman orgy, his general vibe would be 'trip to the dentist'.

Stoicism was, in essence, the world's first 'shut up and deal with it' philosophy. It was perfect for people who saw life as a test. But for anyone who wanted to enjoy the thing, it didn't have much to offer.

But not every school of philosophy was named after a porch. One was named after dogs. Jokingly labelled the *kynikos* – a Greek word meaning 'dog-like' – the Cynics were the world's first anti-establishment dropouts, the first people to take a long, hard look at society and say, 'This shit's not for me.' The original hippies, goths, beatniks or punks. While other Greek philosophers were busy debating what civilisation should look like, the Cynics came to a much simpler conclusion: the very idea was a scam. Comfort was the enemy, convention was a trap, and money, power and relationships were all meaningless crap.

Their answer? Drop out. Go feral. Reject everything. The only way to truly live, they argued, was to be truly free, a state that meant owning nothing, wanting nothing and caring about even less. A good life, for the Cynics, was a life free of dependence, desires, status or shame. If you didn't rely on anything, then nothing could ever hurt you. Their goal was to live as close to nature as possible.

But, much like punk music itself, this sort of thing only sounds good in theory. In practice, it meant sleeping outside, refusing to bathe and really getting to know lots of ticks, mites and fleas. For the Cynics, a life free from social conformity also meant a life free from hygiene. No one modelled this dog-like lifestyle better than Diogenes of Sinope, the most famous Cynic of them all. Possibly not a hit with the ladies, he lived in a barrel in the middle of the Athens marketplace in the 4th century BCE, pooed where he pleased, masturbated in public and wandered around naked, all covered in pee. Other hobbies included accosting strangers at random to tell them their lives were absurd. In the end, the Cynics weren't really trying to enjoy this magical gift called 'life'. They were trying to escape it.

Slightly more welcome in Greek polite society, not least because of his fame as a wrestler, was a heavyset philosopher named Aristocles. Nicknamed 'Plato' (Greek for 'big-shouldered'), he was also a man of big ideas. Responsible for founding a school in Akademia, an Athenian park – and, in so doing, giving us the word 'academic' – Plato was nonetheless another person you probably wouldn't want to invite to a party, unless your plan was to bore all your guests.

If ancient Greece had self-help books, he would have penned titles like *The Life-Changing Magic of Overthinking* and *How to Say Nothing at Length*. His basic schtick, put very crudely, was that the world of abstract ideas and concepts was more real than the world itself. The chair you're sitting on right now, for example, is not actually a chair. It's just an imperfect reflection of 'the idea of chairness'. The bum that you're sitting with? Also a fake, at least compared to a bum's 'Platonic ideal': the concept of perfect 'bumness' that exists somewhere deep in our heads.

Bored yet? If so, that's good, because to Plato, fun was an unnecessary indulgence and an obstacle to intellectual clarity. He found comedy, poetry, wine and theatre all highly suspect. One of his better ideas was to ban poetry.

A good life, in Plato's view, had absolutely nothing to do with enjoyment. It was about the relentless pursuit of wisdom. As he put it, 'The unexamined life is not worth living.' A good life didn't involve messy real-world illusions like sex, snacks or sunsets – it involved abstract reasoning, moral virtue and a highly theoretical understanding of justice that would take me about 683,000 pages to try to explain (and even then, I would get it all wrong). Pleasure muddied the soul. Emotion distracted from the truth. And at the end of the day, the truth was all that really mattered, even if you had to ignore everything enjoyable about being alive to get there.

~

The most famous student at Plato's Akademia was, of course, Aristotle. Probably the most influential philosopher in history (and the personal tutor of Alexander the Great), Aristotle may not have had his mentor's big shoulders, but his brain was a similar size. An authority on logic, biology, politics, poetry, ethics and metaphysics, he had things to say about pretty much every subject – and don't you worry, he was prepared to say them at length.

So what about the subject of happiness? Well, for Aristotle, it wasn't just 'the meaning and the purpose of life'; it was also 'the whole aim and end of human existence'. At first glance, it sounds rather familiar – not unlike something you might find on Instagram. But he didn't mean *our* kind of happiness. More accurately translated as 'flourishing' or 'living well', the Greek word Aristotle used was *eudaimonia*, and it has nothing to do with feeling good.

'The happy life is thought to be virtuous,' he wrote. 'A virtuous life requires exertion and does not consist in amusement.' People obsessed with 'base pleasures', he scoffed, were 'slavish in their tastes', and living 'a life suitable to beasts'. In other words, if your idea of a happy weekend is one spent watching the footy on the couch while inhaling hot chips, Aristotle would not have been impressed. Chances are, he would have confiscated your chips, thrown a rock at your telly and made you write an essay about metaphysics.

In Aristotle's world, *eudaimonia* wasn't a feeling – it was a lifelong project. It was thinking, reasoning and engaging in the noble pursuit of philosophy. You may well ask why. And to be fair, that's an excellent question.

The answer lies in Aristotle's belief that everything in the universe has a purpose, and a 'flourishing' life fulfils it. 'A happy life,' Aristotle said, 'is one that is in accordance with its own nature.' The purpose of an acorn, for example, is to eventually become an oak tree, while the purpose of a knife is to cut. So a happy acorn is one that grows quickly. And a happy knife is a knife that stays sharp.

So what's the purpose of a human being? Simple: reason. Setting aside people who get their facts from Joe Rogan, our ability to think, reflect and act rationally is what sets us apart from plants, animals and rocks. Therefore, to live well – to live happily – is to live in accordance with reason. Just as a good knife cuts well, a good life is led by a person who thinks well. And if you didn't happen to enjoy being 'happy'? Well, too bad.

If you're laughing too much, relaxing too often or choosing pleasure over principle, you're probably doing life wrong. Far better to be miserable and virtuous than comfortable and lazy. Some of Aristotle's more hardcore followers even argued that a truly virtuous person could still be considered 'happy' while being tortured on the rack. Or, I guess, listening to rap.

Now, it's worth mentioning that among all these serious men with their serious beards, ancient Greece also had a few hedonists. They were big fans of prostitutes and were frequently pissed, and their central claim was that physical pleasure is the only intrinsic good and physical pain the only intrinsic bad. All else, including virtue, wisdom and self-discipline, was just unreality. Hedonism was about elevating indulgence to a metaphysical principle.

And for a fleeting moment in history, this idea was taken seriously. Then, an hour or two later, everyone had passed out. Today, hedonism still survives as a word, but as an intellectual school, it didn't last long. While other philosophies inspired empires, hedonism mostly inspired bad hangovers.

So, while the Axial Age thinkers did make a major breakthrough by suggesting humans had some control over their fate, they weren't exactly handing out tips for how to have a good time. Over in the East, Confucius turned happiness into a tedious to-do list, and Buddha dismissed the very concept as flawed. Western philosophers, meanwhile, were more or less united on one thing: happiness wasn't about *feeling* good – it was about *being* good. Suffering wasn't a thing to avoid. In many ways, it was a thing to embrace.

7

GOD ONLY KNOWS

When fun was filed under 'sin'

True happiness is unattainable ...
Mortal life is a kind of hell.

St Augustine, early 5th century

There was a time, not too long ago, when I caught a glimpse of my stomach in a side-view mirror. After collapsing onto the floor, clutching my face and letting out a soft, low moan, I immediately made a solemn vow. It was time to join the gym.

And sure enough, I did just that (albeit a year or so later). Day in and day out, you'd see me in there – complaining, sweating, complaining some more, looking at my phone and occasionally lifting a weight. Combined with a strict diet of no more than three meals a day and just the one glass of wine before lunch, I soon found myself rocking something close to a six-pack (so long as you dimmed all the lights).

But that was then. And this is now. The man writing these words hasn't been to the gym in some time, because those weights are heavy and it's quite a long walk. My six-pack has become a one-pack – or, if you'd prefer, a small keg – and when I finish this sentence, I'll be off for a snack.

Okay, I'm back now. There was a point to that story, believe it or not, and the time has probably come for me to say what it was. Progress, my friends, is not always linear. For every bold step we take toward a brighter, better future, human beings will often take a step back. Or a step sideways. Or a step off a cliff into a dark, raging ocean filled with sharks, rocks and nuclear waste. A person can spend hours spring-cleaning their home, only for it to look like a crime scene by the next day. A country can spend centuries becoming vaguely civilised and then elect Donald Trump.

Entire continents can also fall off a cliff. And there was a point at which Europe did. It all happened during a period that historians now like to call 'Late Antiquity', but which was better known as the 'Dark Ages'.

In the last chapter, we were hanging out with some Greeks around 500 BCE – a classical era full of columns, statues, togas, marble and mansplainers with thick, glossy beards. Well, hot on their sandalled heels came a bunch of Italians who were pretty handy with a siege engine – and were also quite good at stabbing. Starting around 200 BCE, the Romans spent 600 years building the greatest empire the world had ever known. (Though it was less great for any foreigner who didn't like getting stabbed. Or, indeed, spending their life as a slave.)

Still, from the point of view of 'progress', having just one civilisation running the continent had its plus side. Roads, aqueducts, baths, libraries, bridges, ports, sewers, markets and amphitheatres all became fairly commonplace. Literacy spread. Trade boomed. Central heating existed. You could sue someone in the morning, eat honey-glazed lark's tongues for lunch and then spend the afternoon watching gladiators fight a giraffe, while a host of slaves fed you oysters from Gaul.

And then – just like that – you couldn't. It was goodbye *Life of Brian*, hello *Monty Python and the Holy Grail*. One day, people were sipping wine in a bathhouse, chatting about Cicero and maybe making arrangements for a light feast or orgy. The next, they were huddled in a damp, muddy hut alongside three lepers and a cow, hoping a local warlord wouldn't burn down their village.

That, in a nutshell, is what happened when the Roman Empire collapsed in about 476 CE, thanks to a few rampaging tribes with names like the Vandals and Huns. In the space of a few decades, the empire over which the sun never set crumbled into a patchwork of warring fiefdoms, where power belonged to the hairiest maniac with the biggest axe. Without a single, centralised empire to hold things together, Europe became less like a smooth and functional civilisation and more like a Year 9 classroom.

Over time, the more murderous of those maniacs would become dukes, earls and knights – all in service to a king (the most murderous of all). Lords ruled. Vassals obeyed. Serfs worked the fields, got sent off to battle, came down with dysentery and made do with stale bread. The feudal system was born – a brilliantly simple arrangement based on the following principle: 'This land is mine and so is everyone on it. If you don't want to get stabbed, kindly start farming that field. You're all welcome to stop when you're dead.' And so, the Dark Ages began, a time when civilisation switched off the light. Togas were swapped for chainmail. Philosophers gave way to priests. Libraries turned into dungeons. Wealth gave way to poverty. And peace gave way to war.

But the good news, I guess, was that they still had God. Adopted as the official religion of the Roman Empire in the 4th century, Christianity didn't just survive the empire's collapse – it stepped into its shoes. Questioning the Church was about as popular as leprosy and usually a lot more fatal. Kings ruled by *divine right*, which meant God had co-signed their dodgy land grabs and inbred family trees. The aristocracy enforced order with swords and taxes; the Church backed them up with eternal damnation and a confusing menu of indulgences.

It was a monopoly built on fear, superstition and a suspicious number of extremely wealthy bishops.

Education, meanwhile, was strictly for monks, and their curriculum mostly boiled down to the Bible. Monasteries became the medieval equivalent of data centres, with scribes copying scripture by hand, letter by painstaking letter, while the rest of the population tried not to freeze, starve or die of plague. In many villages, the priest was the only literate person, which meant he controlled contracts, confessions, last rites and, if you were lucky, the local rumour mill. By the early medieval period, the Church was Europe's nervous system: school, court, welfare office, news outlet, hospital and postal service.

The world hadn't exactly ended, but if you were a peasant, you probably wished it would. A 'good life' for most people in medieval times was more or less one in which you managed to die of old age, which, at the time, meant about 45. Few would have disagreed with the pope, who summed up existence with all the enthusiasm of a film critic who has just had to sit through some shit from Baz Luhrmann: 'All [people's] days are full of toil and hardship. Rich or poor, master or slave, married or single, good and bad alike – all suffer worldly torments and are tormented by worldly vexations.'

Happiness, in short, wasn't exactly common.

But people wanted it to be, yeah?

Well, nah. As St Bernard of Clairvaux snappily put it, 'The road to hell is paved with joys.'

Up until at least 1500 CE, Christianity was built on pain, sacrifice and the belief that true happiness was not of this earth. The faithful weren't encouraged to enjoy life – they were told to endure it. For medieval Christians, suffering was virtuous. It purified the soul and brought you closer to Christ. God's plan – mysterious, all-powerful and frequently plague-adjacent – had little to do with comfort.

In the dominant Christian worldview, happiness was a reward. And a delayed one at that. It belonged to the next world. The Church didn't promise peace or fulfilment in this life. It promised suffering now in exchange for paradise later. 'This life is not a time of enjoyment,' wrote the 13th-century theologian Thomas à Kempis in *The Imitation of Christ*, 'but of patience and trial.'

Consider Christianity's central symbol: a mutilated corpse nailed to a plank, flanked by weeping women. While other religions chose serene icons – moons, stars, flowers, elegant calligraphy – Team Misery chose an instrument of torture. A device designed to kill slowly, publicly and painfully. As St Therese of Lisieux put it in the 13th century, 'Look upon the cross and learn how sweet is suffering when borne for the Lord.' It's not hard to see why Christianity has often been called 'the worship of sorrow'.

In medieval theology, happiness wasn't the goal. It wasn't even appropriate. Life was a test – a grim, maggot-strewn waiting room, where the truly devout toiled, suffered and obeyed in the hope that enough misery might one day buy them a seat in heaven. Or as St Benedict cheerfully advised, 'Prefer nothing to the love of Christ – not comfort, not laughter, not even your own will.'

And sin, of course, was always lurking nearby. Earthly pleasures were seen as fleeting distractions at best and dangerous temptations at worst. Food? Enjoy it too much and you risk gluttony. Sex? Allowed, technically, but only within marriage, only for procreation and preferably without smiling. Laughter? Be careful – it smelled of pride. Even basic self-esteem was eyed with suspicion.

The seven deadly sins – lust, sloth, pride, greed, envy, wrath, gluttony – sound terrifying until you realise that, aside from the occasional homicide, most of them are just regular ways to enjoy yourself. Sleep in, eat cake, flirt with a stranger, eat more cake – and congratulations, you are halfway to hell. What we might now call basic self-esteem was seen as moral decay.

In this worldview, suffering *was* life. Pain meant progress. Misery meant spiritual growth. Take the Sermon on the Mount, for example – Jesus's most famous speech and, for a while, his best-known. It was addressed to the kinds of people you might now find in the Collingwood cheer squad: the poor, the sick, the smelly and the sad. But instead of urging them to rise up, or even offering a few mental health tips, Jesus said they were blessed. 'Blessed are you who are poor ... who hunger now ... who weep ... who are hated and excluded ... Rejoice in that day and leap for joy, for great is your reward in heaven.'

Translation? If your life sucks, you're doing great. Everything's going according to plan.

But, without wanting to sound like a conspiracy theorist (because, between you and me, those guys are the *worst*), the Church's distrust of pleasure wasn't just about theology. It was also about managing expectations. If people believed happiness was impossible in this life, they were far less likely to complain when their daily reality involved famine, war, lower back pain, itchy wool tunics and shoes made from old wood. By teaching that joy was a sin, the Church helped prop up a social order in which kings ruled by divine right, nobles owned everything, peasants did the work and the Church collected the tithes.

Working hand in hand with landowners – and as Europe's single largest landowner – the Church operated like a spiritual investment scheme: suffer now, obey always and you *might* get eternal bliss. The more miserable you were, the better your odds.

According to historian Helen Parish, 'The Church held a monopoly on salvation, but it was a business too – one that profited from fear, obedience and the promise of something better after death.' In other words, salvation was technically free ... if you paid for it in pain.

To enjoy the world was to risk forgetting your place in it as a lowly, fallen being whose only hope lay in self-denial and divine mercy. Guided by the Church, medieval society leaned hard into the belief that pleasure was dangerous. Not just lust or pride, but anything mildly enjoyable – music, nice clothes, sweet smells, a cheeky jig – was viewed with suspicion. To enjoy the world was to forget your place in it.

The Cistercian monks, for instance, stripped churches of decoration and banned choir singing, fearing it might lure people to sin. By the 13th century, the French were regulating what colours, fabrics and perfumes people could wear, lest anyone get ideas above their station. And then came the bonfires of the vanities: mass burnings of anything considered frivolous or fun. The most infamous took place in 1497, when gigantic crowds torched their mirrors, perfumes, playing cards, paintings and instruments in Florence's central piazza, all in the name of 'purifying' the soul. Thousands cheered as violins cracked and velvet robes burned. One eyewitness described it as 'a pyramid of vanity, four stories high'.

In this light, happiness was potentially heretical. Joy had to wait. The good life came later – in heaven – if you passed the test. And passing the test meant embracing pain, avoiding temptation and never,

ever being too happy. In short, if your life is deeply depressing, then congratulations – you're on the right track.

And if your life didn't happen to be shit? Then maybe it was time to make sure it was. Much like fans of St Kilda Football Club, many medieval Christians actively sought out suffering – actively chose a life of torture and pain. Monks and nuns, in particular, would often starve themselves, flog themselves or go without sleep to underline their devotion and, in the process, get closer to God. The more miserable you were, the holier you became. If salvation required hardship, the logic went, then why not get a head start?

Take the medieval hairshirt, a fashion disaster rivalled only by mullets. Made from coarse animal hair (and ideally infested with fleas), the shirt was designed to be itchy, scratchy and uncomfortable enough to drive you halfway to madness. The best ones came with needles.

But other martyrs thought that scratchy shirts were for wusses. They wanted serious wounds. Enter the Flagellants: groups of hardcore penitents who roamed the streets of Europe in the Middle Ages, lashing their backs with a whip. 'They beat themselves with scourges,' one chronicler observed, 'so that the blood ran down in streams and they groaned and wept bitterly ... Some flogged themselves until the bones lay bare.'

St Catherine of Siena, an Italian mystic canonised in 1461, was another master of self-inflicted misery. Fond of going without food for weeks at a time, she wore an iron-spiked chain wrapped tightly around her body and slept on a wooden plank.

Not to be outdone, St Rose of Lima wore a metal crown lined with inward-facing spikes and regularly rubbed her face with hot peppers. And just to make sure she wasn't enjoying life too much, she also slept on a mattress made of broken glass. Her spiritual advisor described her as 'a rose grown among thorns, whose fragrance was pain'. I myself would say she was a lunatic.

Equally excited about the magical gift that is life were the Stylites, Christian ascetics who chose to live for decades on top of tall stone pillars. The most famous was St Simeon Stylites, who, in the 5th century, reportedly stayed on his pillar for 37 years, tying himself to it with ropes that eventually grew into his flesh.

Then you have the Anchorites of the Middle Ages. They chose to live permanently walled into tiny, windowless cells, often with a priest bricking them in during a formal ceremony. What they did for a toilet is lost to history, but I suspect it came with a smell.

I could go on and on. So I think I will. Celebrated today as the patron saint of animals, St Francis of Assisi was better known in the 13th century for rolling around naked in the snow to suppress lustful thoughts and refusing to see a doctor as he went slowly blind. He also gave himself quite a few deep, bloody wounds on his feet and wrists to match those borne by Christ on the cross.

In so doing, he was not unlike a certain German Dominican friar, Blessed Henry Suso, the most popular vernacular writer of the 14th century, who carved Jesus's name into his chest, wore an iron cross covered in nails and designed a 'discipline belt' full of needles and spikes.

Around the same time, St Lutgardis of Aywières, a Belgian medieval saint, fell deeply, chronically ill – but, just like an anti-vaxxer, rejected every doctor's attempt at a cure. When she eventually went blind as well, she thanked God for the bonus, calling it a 'gift of suffering that freed her from the distractions of the visible world'.

A good matchmaker would have set her up with St Benedict Joseph Labre, an 18th-century French ascetic who wandered from shrine to shrine dressed in rags and covered in sores and refusing any shelter or food. When he died, his stench was reportedly so strong that it cleared out the streets. Nothing in Paris would stink so badly again until the premiere of *Amélie* in 2001.

So the next time your couch feels a little too firm, spare a thought for the Christians of old. They were living in a world that actively encouraged misery and self-torment, a world in which the meekest were blessed. It was a deeply weird philosophy, but it was deeply ingrained in the culture. The pursuit of happiness was not.

8

LOSING MY RELIGION

How the Enlightenment ushered in the age of happiness

It matters not how strait the gate,
How charged with punishments the scroll,
I am the master of my fate,
I am the captain of my soul.

William Henley, *Invictus*, 1875

Here's a question for you, dear reader. What is history's most important invention? The wheel? The internet? Antibiotics? Electricity? If you put ten academics in a room, you'll end up with ten different answers (provided you resist the temptation to set it on fire).

If you ask me, I'm tempted to say Pantene two-in-one shampoo and conditioner. But for the purposes of this chapter, I'll pick something else. Because if there's one moment that truly shook up civilisation, it was the invention of a clunky, chunky, gear-laden contraption containing cranks, pulleys, screws, levers and plates.

Before the printing press came along in the mid-15th century, literacy was about as common in Europe as a fair trial for the village witch. You'd find more general knowledge in the average AFL cheer squad than you would in the average city. And if, by some miracle, you were able to read a book, you also had to be miraculously rich in order to find one. The medieval equivalent of a Ferrari, books were a rare and special luxury item, painstakingly copied out by hand, letter by letter, line by line, over months or years. And since most scribes were monks, the overwhelming majority of books were bibles. Or commentaries on the Bible. Or books about saints. Or lists of the many ways in which man could sin.

Enter Johannes Gutenberg: a debt-riddled, slightly dodgy German entrepreneur who'd previously made a living flogging 'holy mirrors'. But Johannes wasn't just an ideas man; he was also an excellent metalworker. In the 1440s, he put those skills to use by creating a machine that could mass-produce print. In other words, he built the first printer. He then lost the patent to one of his creditors and ended his days homeless and broke.

But Johannes at least had the comfort of seeing his idea start to change the world. Within fifty years, printing presses had sprung up in over 250 European cities. Within another century, tens of millions of books were in circulation – and not all of them were bibles. The West now had pamphlets, plays, polemics, personal letters, anatomical diagrams, legal codes, travelogues, almanacs, maps and manifestos. Basically, if it could be inked, it was printed.

After a millennium of mostly being ignored, ancient Greek and Roman texts were rediscovered, dusted off, translated, printed and passed around like intellectual contraband. New schools and universities began to pop up all over the place, and suddenly scholars were quoting Aristotle over breakfast and arguing about Plato in pubs. Once a continent of chronic illiteracy, Europe found itself drowning in information.

The printing press was, in essence, the internet of its time – just with far fewer cat videos and considerably less porn. It was nothing short of a cultural earthquake, a beam of light that helped put an end to the so-called 'Dark Ages', blasting open the gates of knowledge that had long been chained shut. The result was an intellectual rebirth (or a 'Renaissance', to use the French term), and I'm not just talking about a bunch of artists poncing about in tights or chiselling statues with reassuringly small penises. I'm talking about a full-blown resurrection of classical ideals: reason, science, beauty, civic virtue, critical inquiry.

For more than a thousand years, the Church had essentially closed the door on independent thought. But now, the gates had been flung open. Suddenly, facts and ideas weren't the exclusive property of kings, lords and priests. They could be duplicated. Shared. Read in bed. The printing press reignited the Western passion for thinking. And it spread faster than a rash at an orgy.

But here's the problem with thinking, my friends. It generally leads to doubts. As books, journals and pamphlets spread new ideas all over Europe, more and more people – farmers, merchants, scholars and, yes, even women – began to ask more and more questions. Was it possible, some wondered, that joy wasn't sinful? That life might actually have more to offer than faith, fear and warts? That God didn't want us to be meek?

Never one to mince his words, Niccolò Machiavelli was one of the first to spell this out in cold, cynical ink. 'Fortune is a woman,' he charmingly declared, 'and if you wish to keep her under control, you must beat her and bully her.' Fate, in other words, favours the bold. Don't sit around praying for mercy. Take action. Seize the day. Grab life by the throat. And if you get the chance, try to stab a few rivals.

Slightly less violent but just as subversive was a French nobleman named Michel de Montaigne. His *Essays*, first published in 1580, posited the revolutionary notion that life didn't have to be total shit. 'The most certain sign of wisdom is cheerfulness,' he wrote, a line that would have made any self-respecting monk spill cold gruel on his hair shirt. Pleasure, curiosity and even laughter were not moral failures. You didn't have to flog yourself for trying to have fun.

And then there was François Rabelais, a French doctor, priest, prankster, alcoholic, food-enthusiast and all-round bad boy. His wild, sprawling 16th-century novels were stuffed with semen, farts and shitfaced monks, but beneath the chaos was a celebration of joy. Why sit around waiting for salvation, he asked, when you could eat, drink, laugh, shag? Why endure life when you could actually enjoy it?

The Renaissance was, in short, a revolution of perspective. Where once holiness was measured in misery, a growing number of thinkers were suggesting that maybe – just maybe – happiness was not a trap set by the devil, but a sign you were doing something right.

But when it comes to controversial writers whose words changed the world, there's no going past Martin Luther. A grumpy German law student who became a grumpy German monk, Luther suffered from chronic guilt, kidney stones and crippling constipation.

But his chief problem, so to speak, were the popes. Specifically, popes like 10th-century John XII, who gambled, drank, slept with his relatives, turned the Vatican into a 'brothel' and died in bed with another man's wife. And Benedict IX, who was accused of rape, murder and various 'unspeakable acts'. And Stephen VI, who dug up a dead predecessor, propped the corpse up in court and put it on trial. And, of course, Alexander VI, whose CV included bribery, nepotism, murder, incest and throwing a banquet for fifty prostitutes.

Luther was also less than impressed with Catholic corruption in general. With the way priests blessed kings, propped up barons and preached obedience from the pulpit while hoarding land, wealth and power and shagging their nieces. With the way bishops lived like lords, friars slept around, inquisitors tortured heretics and monks sold salvation.

So, in 1517, Luther said no to yet another helping of bratwurst and got to work picking a fight with the Church. Seemingly unbothered by the idea of spending eternity roasting in hell, he went on to publish ninety-five very punchy critiques. But despite zingers like 'Rome is the fountain of all filthiness' and 'I despise and attack it as false, impious and satanic', Luther's aim had simply been to spark some light reform and maybe get a few monks to cut back spending on brothels.

What he got instead was a full-blown revolution. Thanks to the printing press, his Ninety-Five Theses spread across Europe like wildfire, finding eager readers in taverns, castles and huts. And they brought with them an idea that – up until that point – had been unthinkable. What if the pope didn't actually know everything about everything?

For over a thousand years, His Holiness had been nothing less than God's right-hand man. Infallible, untouchable and unbelievably terrifying, since he alone held the keys to salvation. The pope alone interpreted the words of the Bible. The pope alone could interpret God's plan. If he said you were going to hell, then you were going to hell. All that remained was to die.

But once Luther cracked open that door of doubt, a flood came pouring through. Not just from monks and peasants, but from kings, queens, merchants, philosophers – anyone who'd ever been forced to cough up their last halfpenny, florin, ducat or mark to pay for yet another fucking church roof.

Because if the Pope could be wrong ... what might be right? Could salvation really be bought? Did you need a priest to speak to God? Could ordinary people read the Bible for themselves, in their own language, without a Latin-speaking middleman? Could faith be a quiet, personal, individual thing, not something decreed and defined by a big institution?

The movement that followed became known as Protestantism. And protest is exactly what they did. Protestants weren't just founding new churches – they were openly rebelling against the old one. They didn't just reject indulgences; they rejected the whole idea that truth, salvation and grace had to be bought, licensed or approved by Rome. As Luther himself put it, 'Every man is his own priest ... the Holy Scripture is the only faithful teacher of all godliness and virtue.'

What began in 1517 with a grumpy monk quickly escalated into a full-blown spiritual revolution. New branches of Christianity sprang up across Europe: Lutherans, Calvinists, Anabaptists, Anglicans – each with their own views on scripture, sin, sacraments and salvation.

In the short term, it meant chaos. Bloody wars. Torture. Excommunications. Massacres. Entire nations tore themselves apart. Families split. Thousands were burned at the stake. But the fuse had been lit: the radical idea that you could challenge authority – and live – had entered the bloodstream of Europe.

The Reformation didn't just shake up religion – it cracked the foundations of Western thought. Suddenly, truth wasn't something handed down from on high by popes, kings or ancient tradition. It wasn't locked in Latin or guarded by clergy. Now, truth could be found in the individual soul. In study. In reason. In conscience.

The Bible stayed on the shelf, but now it had company: telescopes, microscopes, anatomical diagrams, treatises, manifestos, proofs scribbled in candlelight. And once people stopped worrying about being burned at the stake, they started to ask some big questions. Big, dangerous questions. What is nature? Who holds power? What *is* truth? Enter Galileo, Descartes, Newton, Bacon: brainy men with a whole new mindset. Men who weren't prepared to wait for answers from above but who tried to find out for themselves. In the stars. In the blood. In the physics of falling apples.

The universe, it turned out, wasn't a divine riddle. It was a machine. And with the right tools, you could see how it ticked.

But the Reformation's long-term consequences were even more seismic. As German sociologist Max Weber famously argued, Protestantism reshaped faith and rewired the psychological and economic foundations of the modern West. The core shift was this: under Catholicism, your relationship with God was mediated by priests, rituals and a rigid Church hierarchy. You were part of a flock – obedient, sacramental, low in rank.

French 20th-century anthropologist Louis Dumont put it this way: 'In traditional society, the individual was born into a fixed place in a social order. His duties and identity were prescribed by custom and religion.' American historian Christopher Lasch added that man 'saw himself as part of a larger order – cosmic, social and religious'.

Protestantism blew that model apart. Suddenly, every soul stood alone before God. No intercessors. No infallible pope. Just you, your Bible and your conscience. Religion was no longer housed in cathedrals – it lived in conduct, personal discipline, a life well lived.

After the Reformation, the individual began to matter. Faith, once mediated by church bells and incense, became a quiet and often terrifying dialogue between the individual and God. The soul was now a DIY project.

So what did people do? Well, next up on our whistle-stop tour of Western thought is an era we now call the Enlightenment: a dazzling age of science, liberty, encyclopaedias, revolutions and rather rotund, pompous men with big wigs. Largely unfolding in the 17th and 18th centuries, the Enlightenment was the golden age of polymaths and prodigies. Robert Hooke was peering through microscopes, Christopher Wren was redesigning half of London, Isaac Newton was inventing calculus and Luigi Galvani was making frogs' legs dance with electricity. These weren't just eccentric hobbies – they were the early tremors of the modern world. A world full of IT experts, engineers and tedious men who like to talk about cars. Science was starting to take the place of religion. Truth was now observable, testable and up for debate.

But forget the scientists; let's stick with the philosophers. Because at the heart of the Enlightenment lay a truly scandalous idea. An idea so dark, so twisted, so dangerously radical it might as well have involved necrophilia. Here goes: happiness was good. The French revolutionary Louis Antoine de Saint put it more bluntly: 'Happiness is a new idea in Europe.'

Yes, happiness. Not in the next life. Not as a reward for your suffering. But in the here and now. Suddenly, it wasn't greedy to want comfort. It wasn't sinful to smile, laugh, eat well or enjoy looking good. Pleasure wasn't a trap or a temptation – it was a right. For the first time in Western history, joy wasn't just for powdered aristocrats or the occasional pagan. It was for everyone. It was something ordinary people had a right to pursue.

John Locke – a mild-mannered 17th-century English doctor-turned-'father of liberalism' – helped kick off the whole shebang. 'The business of man is to be happy in this world,' he declared. In *An Essay Concerning Human Understanding*, he argued that 'the highest perfection of intellectual nature lies in a careful and constant pursuit of true and solid happiness'. That pursuit wasn't selfish – it was natural, rational, even noble.

Then there was Denis Diderot, the creator of the first encyclopaedia, a book swiftly banned by both Louis XV and Pope Clement XIII. In its pages, he quietly lobbed a grenade: 'Does not everyone have a right to happiness according to his whims?' And the logical next step? That governments should have a role in providing it.

For most of history, power had flowed in one direction: downward. Rather like my old boss, Janine, kings and popes had ruled under the assumption that their authority came straight from God. That to question their right to rule was both illegal and blasphemous. You may as well spit straight into God's mouth or knee him right in the balls.

But Enlightenment thinkers flipped this script. They argued that happiness could be engineered. That misery wasn't a fixed part of the human condition. Get the political structures right, put smart social policies in place, give people education, legal protections and economic freedom, and suffering became optional.

Thanks to figures like Locke, Voltaire, Montesquieu and Rousseau, the right to happiness began to move from crazy idea to political blueprint. It became the gold standard of policymaking and the foundational principle of modern political thought. All over Europe and across the Atlantic, governments were increasingly expected to create the conditions in which citizens could pursue joy.

Not only that – it was their job. Government, Locke insisted, wasn't 'the will of the sovereign'; it was a trust. A social contract between the ruled and their rulers. 'Whenever the legislators endeavour to take away and destroy the property of the people,' he wrote, 'they put themselves into a state of war with the people.' And if some inbred prince with webbed feet didn't stick to his part of the deal, then the people had every right to replace him. Peacefully, if possible; violently if necessary. The age of divine right was over. The age of human rights had arrived.

One of its loudest American cheerleaders was a lanky redhead from rural Virginia. Endlessly curious and even more racist, President Thomas Jefferson was more or less the Enlightenment in human form. He designed and built his own mansion, collected fossils, invented gadgets, experimented with vegetables, owned over 6000 books ... and about 600 human beings.

When this young statesman drafted the Declaration of Independence in 1776, he didn't just borrow one of John Locke's phrases about man's right to 'life, liberty and property'. He upgraded it. Out went 'property' and in came something loftier. 'We hold these truths to be self-evident, that all men are created equal, that they are endowed by their Creator with certain unalienable Rights, that among these are Life, Liberty and the pursuit of Happiness.' Of course, that pursuit only really applied to white, land-owning male voters like himself. But it seems fair to say that the phrase stuck.

No longer was happiness a divine indulgence or the fleeting result of good luck. Pursuing it was now a right. A right that citizens could expect (if they had the right skin colour) and a right that their governments should protect.

And if a leader didn't protect that right? Well, just ask King Louis XVI. Kicking off in 1789 with the Storming of the Bastille, the French Revolution was a blood-soaked whirlwind of famine, debt, inequality, war, rage, baguettes, pâté and social collapse. After killing pretty much every aristo they could find, revolutionaries started killing each other, only to take their turn. Much like the remake of *Dirty Dancing*, it was a spectacular, and unforgivable, mess. But beneath all the severed heads lay something recognisably modern: a refusal to accept that misery was mankind's natural state.

As radical journalist Jean-Paul Marat thundered (before being stabbed to death in his bath in 1793), 'The people have a right to happiness. And the tyrants have no right to the people.' Revolutionary firebrand Georges Danton was equally blunt before he too was guillotined: 'We ask that the people be given the means to enjoy the fruits of their labour, that they be assured of their rights and that happiness be within their reach.'

But perhaps no one took the cause of happiness more seriously – or more disturbingly – than Maximilien Robespierre. Known as 'the Incorruptible', Robespierre saw himself as the custodian of *le bonheur public* – public happiness. In a 1794 speech to the National Convention, he declared, 'The aim of constitutional government is to preserve the Republic; the aim of republican government is to bring about the reign of virtue; the aim of virtue is to ensure the happiness of the people.'

For Robespierre, happiness was a right and a duty. And if achieving mass happiness required mass executions, so be it. Under his leadership, the Reign of Terror saw over 16,000 people guillotined in the name of public happiness. Eventually, of course, the public decided they'd be happier still if Robespierre got the chop too.

Over in England, meanwhile, things were rather less revolutionary, but happiness certainly had no shortage of advocates. The most prominent was probably Jeremy Bentham, an English social reformer whose stuffed and mummified body can still be seen at University College in London, along with the homemade walking sticks he named 'Judy' and 'Dapple'. Widely considered the father of utilitarianism (and, while we're at it, a bit of a weirdo), Bentham didn't just argue that happiness was the most important consideration for government. He argued that it was the *only* important consideration for government. Forget about bibles or laws or royals or rights, said Jezza. 'The value of a state is measured by the happiness of its people ... It is the greatest happiness of the greatest number that is the measure of right and wrong.'

Bentham's intellectual heir, John Stuart Mill, put it even more succinctly: 'Actions are right in proportion as they tend to promote happiness; wrong as they tend to produce the reverse.' It was, in effect, morality by spreadsheet. List possible outcomes, add up the joy and subtract the misery. No need to consult a priest; just do the maths.

By the time the Enlightenment had more or less wrapped up (leaving behind a shiny new country called America and a pile of dead Frenchmen), the idea that happiness was somehow unholy was starting to look a bit passé. Among Protestants, more and more theologians began branding Christianity not as a preparation for paradise but as a potential way to enjoy it on Earth. Happiness, they argued, wasn't necessarily always a trap set by Satan. Done right, it could actually be a sign of virtue. As the English 18th-century founder of Methodism, John Wesley, put it, 'True religion is right tempers towards God and man. It is in two words: gratitude and benevolence. And it is happiness itself.' Thomas Jefferson echoed his point (probably before going off to shag one of his slaves): 'Virtue and happiness are intimately connected.'

Even in the Catholic world, where masochism had long been the house special, things were beginning to shift. In the late 19th century, Pope Leo XIII declared, 'True happiness is found not in riches or pleasures, but in the virtues.' The old dichotomy of holy or happy was beginning to look like a false choice. You could be good and feel good ... so long as your joy was grounded in faith, family, humility and hard work. Happiness wasn't necessarily a temptation to resist. Under the right conditions, it was something to aspire to. Happiness was still wrapped in robes of Christian duty, but compared to the medieval ideal of weeping, toiling and bleeding your way to heaven, this was a revolution.

Gutenberg's printing press, in short, shattered the sanctity of misery. Within a few hundred years of its first print run, happiness had stopped being sinful, selfish or at the very least suspicious. It had become, more or less, the whole point.

9

I ME MINE

How we all became obsessed with ourselves

The pursuit of your own happiness
is the only moral purpose of your life.

Ayn Rand, *Atlas Shrugged*, 1957

Sky News pundits. Lifestyle influencers. Colour consultants. The world is full of well-paid professions that, to me, add nothing of value. Professions that, in the cold light of day, make it hard to believe capital punishment is wrong. To my mind, economists also belong on that list (just below people who work in PR). It's not that economists don't have anything to say. It's that they seem to have everything to say. Which, in practice, means they say nothing at all. Take any given event – say, interest rates rising or a fall in unemployment – and you'll find at least three economists calling it good news, three saying it's bad and another six saying it all depends. Every opinion is delivered with the same quiet authority, scientific precision and complicated series of graphs. It's like having a dozen different bureaus of meteorology, each one offering a different forecast, and each one always wrong.

And yet, just as my home printer occasionally works and not every Zoom meeting is a complete waste of time, there are times when an economist says something that they don't have to retract the next day. The last time this happened was in 1776.

Writing at the very height of the Enlightenment – think heaving bosoms, pistols at dawn, rakes, bucks and packed pantaloons – a slightly awkward academic from Edinburgh published a book that continues to shape global thought to this day. At the time, you see, most people believed that wealth was a zero-sum game. That if one person got rich, someone else had to get poor. The economy was like a pie that only came in one fixed size. The only question was how to slice it.

But in *The Wealth of Nations*, the 'father of capitalism' proposed something revolutionary: that self-interest was a sort of yeast-like ingredient that, if encouraged, could help the pie grow. Adam Smith argued that when people help themselves, they unintentionally help others too. 'It is not from the benevolence of the butcher, the brewer, or the baker that we expect our dinner,' he wrote, 'but from their regard to their own interest.'

In other words, you don't need everyone to be kind and generous; you just need them to look after themselves. So if governments created a system that better rewarded hard work, everyone would ultimately benefit, even if that wasn't the butcher's intention. Smith called this self-interest the 'invisible hand' – a slightly creepy bit of economic poetry suggesting that market forces, if left alone, could guide us all to the common good.

Seen in this light, self-interest wasn't selfish. It was a public service. A rising tide that could lift all boats. In time, this idea became the cornerstone of capitalism. And (setting aside centuries of inequality, exploitation, war, debt, stress, obesity and environmental destruction), it's fair to say it's worked pretty well.

But Smith's big idea – that greed was good – didn't just reshape the Western economy; it rewired the Western mind. For most of human history, identity was something you were assigned. You belonged to a tribe, kin group, caste or parish and played your role in it so all could survive. The world was precarious, brutal and cold. Community was your heating system, food supply and security plan, all rolled into one.

Wins were shared. So were losses. The idea of 'making it on your own' would've sounded as strange as having a bath, or liking someone from France. And if you started muttering some nonsense about 'finding yourself', your neighbours would've assumed you'd been kicked by a horse.

Then came capitalism, a system that didn't just reward individualism but demanded it. As Canadian philosopher Charles Taylor put it, 'Where once people saw themselves as inseparable from their neighbours, the family and the divine order, the rise of capitalism and Enlightenment thought encouraged them to view themselves as autonomous agents, responsible for their own destiny.'

In a world where wealth could now be created, not just inherited, people were told to go out and earn it. Your fate was no longer fixed by your surname, parish or social class. You could buy land, open a shop, write a manifesto or reinvent yourself entirely. You weren't expected to blend into family, church or community. You were expected to stand out, to compete, to win.

Everyone, in theory, could rise. Everyone, in theory, could win. And even if you hadn't won yet, the belief that you might was enough to keep you compliant, hopeful and busy, building your dream, paying your taxes and blaming yourself when things didn't quite pan out.

As markets expanded and capitalism spread, something subtle shifted. You were no longer just Egbert the Butcher – you were Egbert Pty Ltd, an independent small business. You didn't just sell rancid mutton and three-week-old pig's trotters. You sold your time, your skills and your labour. Just like the contents of your meat pies, life was a project that you could design for yourself.

Few people today would reject capitalism outright or deny that some degree of self-interest is in the interest of all. Whether or not we believe 'there is no such thing as society', as Margaret Thatcher once declared, many of us behave as if it were true. Western life rarely revolves around tradition or fitting into a community. It's all about forging your own path.

Capitalism, in short, created a new kind of person: the autonomous, self-interested individual. A person who didn't wait to be chosen. A person who chose themselves. Slowly but surely, the rugged individual became the central character of Western life. Not the churchgoer. Not the nobleman. Not the obedient peasant. The self-made man who owed success to himself.

And nowhere was the gospel of individualism more devoutly preached – or more aggressively monetised – than in the Land of Opportunity. Or, if you prefer, the Land of the Free. Within decades of *The Wealth of Nations* hitting the shelves, the American frontier was teeming with farmers, fur traders, land-grabbers, gold-diggers and immigrants of every stripe. In a land where aristocratic titles meant nothing and family crests were mostly imaginary, the individual became king.

In 1831, a young French aristocrat named Alexis de Tocqueville set sail for the United States. Officially, he was there to study the prison system. Unofficially, he was trying to work out what the fuck was going on in this strange new democracy across the sea, a society with no kings, no inherited titles and a weird number of motivational slogans. What struck him most about the New World was its psychology. Americans, he observed, had embraced what he called 'the charm of anticipated success', that relentless, hopeful, slightly deranged belief that anything was possible with hustle.

But beneath the optimism, de Tocqueville detected a nervous twitch, a kind of spiritual FOMO. A 'feverish ardour' in the pursuit of prosperity and a 'vague dread' that they might not be taking the fastest route to get there. 'They clutch everything,' he wrote, 'they hold nothing fast, but soon loosen their grasp to pursue fresh gratifications.' Even surrounded by comforts, Americans seemed haunted by the idea that some greater happiness might be slipping through their fingers, possibly on the next wagon, in the next goldmine or behind the next slightly better rocking chair.

The result, de Tocqueville concluded, was a 'strange melancholy ... in the midst of abundance'. 'In the United States,' he wrote, 'I have seen the freest and most enlightened men placed in the happiest circumstances that the world affords ... and I thought them serious and almost sad even in their pleasures ... They are much more excited by hope than by possession; and this sometimes renders them insensible to actual enjoyment. The result is that they clutch everything without satisfaction.'

By the mid-19th century, the self-made myth had gone full paperback thanks to American author Horatio Alger, whose eighty billion or so novels all told the same basic story: plucky orphan meets kindly millionaire, works hard, makes it big. These weren't just bedtime stories – they were bedtime theology. In this new gospel of capitalism, captains of industry were both rich and righteous. Steel industrialist Andrew Carnegie started in a Scottish hovel and ended up with enough money to buy Scotland itself. John D Rockefeller began as a humble bookkeeper and wound up controlling America's oil. Both men swore their empires were built on thrift, discipline and Christian values, though those values also seemed to include union-busting, monopolies, starvation wages, rampant corruption and the occasional threat or bribe.

Success, in this framework, was part of a much larger cultural sales pitch. Your job might be soul-crushing, your hours might be inhuman and your tiny hovel might be infested with rats. But if you worked hard and kept your nose clean, sooner or later you'd get ahead.

But self-interest didn't just give us self-made men; it also gave us self-absorption. As de Tocqueville famously sniffed, 'Each citizen is habitually engaged in the contemplation of a very puny object, namely himself.' The more we celebrated the self as the engine of progress, the more that self demanded attention. The big question was no longer 'How should I live in the world?' but 'What does the world mean to me?' What began as a culture of personal responsibility – work hard, be self-reliant, forge your path – gradually morphed into the culture we now have today. A culture in which every second person likes to bang on about their own 'journey' and fondly imagines it to be a story unlike any heard before. A culture where it's apparently no longer enough to simply *live* a good life. You also have to analyse it, photograph it, hashtag it, brand it and write about it at length.

Barring a few ancient exceptions (I'm looking at you, Marcus Aurelius), the literary culture of self-absorption really took off with Jean-Jacques Rousseau, an Enlightenment philosopher and one of history's first oversharers. In *Confessions* (1782), he declared, 'I am not made like any of those I have seen; I dare believe I am not made like any of those who are in existence.' Then he spent 700 pages proving it, including his fondness for being spanked by aristocrats and flashing women in public. No detail was too small or shameful. No passing thought did not need to be heard.

By the 1800s, the torch had passed to Lord Byron, arguably the first 'celebrity' in the modern sense of 'shameless attention-seeker'. Fond of incest, opium, rent boys, debt, exotic animals and other men's wives, Byron wasn't just mad, bad and dangerous to know; he was also madly self-absorbed. 'I am such a strange mélange of good and evil,' sighed this dark and brooding outsider, probably while gazing into a mirror. His most famous poem, 'Childe Harold's Pilgrimage', is essentially a 300-page autobiography featuring a world-weary young aristocrat wandering Europe in search of meaning and instead finding sexy widows. Every stanza depicts Harold sulking in a picturesque location because no one understands him. Byron didn't just invent the Byronic hero; he *was* the Byronic hero: aloof, tortured, magnetic, scandalous. And – after a while – kind of tedious.

Oscar Wilde was cut from the same cloth, famously announcing in 1891 that 'the individual is the only reality. The community is a fabrication of the mind.' It was around this time that diaries – once the quiet domain of monks and misfits – became performance pieces. The personal became literary. Enter the age of the memoir, the confessional essay, the blog, the podcast, Facebook and the Instagram story about what you just had for breakfast and whether or not you planned to skip lunch. As Wilde put it, 'I never travel without my diary. One should always have something sensational to read on the train.'

Nowhere was this turn inward more obvious than in the novel. In the 18th century, fiction gave us dragons, knights and swooning heroines. By the 19th, the action had slowed to a polite crawl. Heroes, gods and monsters were out; in came sensitive misfits with too much time on their hands. Plot took a back seat to psychology. Characters wandered windswept estates, fretted over social slights and suffered seven-page internal crises over whether to say 'hello' at a dinner party. Entire chapters were devoted to the quiet torment of choosing a cravat.

By the early 20th century, things got even more inward-looking. The 'stream of consciousness' novel turned introspection into an art form and, frankly, a bit of a chore. James Joyce's *Ulysses* gave us 700 pages of unpunctuated thought spirals, while Marcel Proust spent more than 1.2 million words exploring the curious workings of memory and whether or not he was feeling up to dinner. Count Leo Tolstoy wrote about the spiritual torment of rich men in waistcoats, while Virginia Woolf gave us internal monologues, Franz Kafka bureaucratic nightmares and Jean-Paul Sartre a novel whose main character mostly thinks about chairs.

And so the modern literary hero was born. He wasn't a warrior, a hero or even a villain, but a neurotic, underemployed overthinker with a rich inner life. All this introspection brought nuance, yes, but also a new affliction: a world full of people endlessly gazing at their own navels, convinced that all meaning and purpose must lie somewhere within.

10

MONEY CHANGES EVERYTHING

How we swapped salvation for shopping

If we command our wealth, we shall be rich and free.
If our wealth commands us, we are poor indeed.
Edmund Burke, *Letters on a Regicide Peace*, 1796

Remember the first Agricultural Revolution 10,000 years ago? (Don't worry, I'm not angry if you don't, but I do have to say I'm a little hurt. We covered it in Chapter 3.) As historical tsunamis go, that one had only one real rival: the Industrial Revolution: a wave of steel, sparks, smoke and soot that began in Britain and slowly spread its way over the West.

Before 1780 or thereabouts, towns and cities were small. The vast majority of people lived on farms or in tiny villages, sowed and ploughed fields and measured their wealth in sheep, turnips or cows. The economy was small, stagnant and largely dependent on the season, give or take the occasional drought.

But then everything changed. The first sparks of the Machine Age were lit in 1764, when an English carpenter named James Hargreaves invented a machine that allowed a single worker to spin multiple spools of thread. His 'spinning jenny' was soon followed by Richard Arkwright's water frame, Samuel Crompton's spinning mule and Edmund Cartwright's power loom – inventions that let every Tom, Dick and Harry crank out clothes, blankets and sails faster than ever before.

Meanwhile, a Scotsman named James Watt was tinkering with steam engines and, in the process, reshaping the planet. By improving the engine's efficiency, he freed industries from their reliance on rivers. Because they were no longer tied to water wheels, factories could now be built anywhere – and run for as long as workers could be kept awake. 'Steam is an Englishman,' declared the German poet Heinrich Heine, 'it thinks for him, it moves for him, it executes his will.'

This wasn't just an economic shift. It was a full-blown social revolution. The countryside emptied as millions of peasants swapped ploughs for payslips, chasing the promise of steady wages in smoke-choked cities. Manchester, Birmingham and Glasgow swelled from sleepy market towns into industrial behemoths. London's population ballooned from one to six million and the skyline began to bristle with chimneys.

Improvements to coal-powered blast furnaces meant iron could now be churned out in unprecedented quantities, fuelling the birth of bridges, railways and steamships. Meanwhile, the telegraph shrank communication time from months to minutes and gas lighting began illuminating homes and streets. As one Londoner put it, 'It's like having daylight on tap.' Productivity no longer stopped at sunset – and neither did anything else. Evening theatre, cafe society and late-night strolls (and, naturally, late-night crime) all flourished under the glow of gaslight.

Now, the Industrial Revolution obviously had its fair share of downsides. Much like my local fish and chip shop, the 1800s had some truly horrific working conditions, the kind that would make any self-respecting millennial resign in under a second and then sue for emotional damage. I'm talking about fourteen-hour shifts in cramped, smoky rooms with no windows and absolutely no sick days. I'm talking safety standards being just not a thing. If you lost a finger in the machinery, the main concern of a Victorian boss was said finger potentially jamming the gears. And that's without even mentioning the coal mines, where little kids dragged carts of coal through long, cold, damp and pitch-black tunnels, along with a nasty case of black lung.

But the age of invention didn't just invent terrible working conditions; it also gave us pollution and slums. As Karl Marx's chum Friedrich Engels wrote, 'workers live[d] in the most wretched, filthy and ruinous houses imaginable'. Open sewers crisscrossed urban streets. Cholera outbreaks were a standard affair and tuberculosis did a brisk trade. At one point, the Thames became so clogged with shit that the House of Commons had to be abandoned.

But enough of this bleeding-heart lefty whinging. Margaret Thatcher would be turning in her grave, if she wasn't busy burning in hell. Because, all things considered – it's pretty hard to escape the conclusion that, for most Westerners, life got much better. Before the Industrial Revolution, the idea of 'progress' had been mostly theoretical, a topic discussed in salons by posh men in wigs when they weren't busy groping the waitress. But the 19th century was different. It was an era in which the quality of life measurably improved for huge swathes of the population.

The English writer Walter Bagehot marvelled at the change, noting that 'the middle of the 19th century saw a new creature rise in the world: the ordinary man, comfortably fed'. Bread, once brown and coarse, was now white and sliced. Tea replaced gin as the national drink.

Meanwhile, medicine had leapt from total guesswork to partial guesswork. English physician Edward Jenner's smallpox vaccine, introduced in 1796, began saving lives on an unprecedented scale, and by the mid-19th century, vaccination programs were spreading across Europe. Antiseptics, pioneered by British surgeon Joseph Lister in the 1860s, transformed surgery from a bloody horror show into something resembling actual healthcare. 'It is not the knife, but the dirt,' Lister insisted, 'that kills the patient.'

Sanitation also began to catch up with science. As cities grew and cholera outbreaks mounted, it finally dawned on local governments that open cesspits and sewage-strewn streets were not, in fact, signs of progress. London's 1858 'Great Stink' – when the smell of raw sewage on the Thames grew so unbearable it shut down half the city – prompted a flurry of public health reforms. Modern sewer systems were built, waste was carted away and drinking water was (mostly) separated from shit.

To be clear, Victorian cities were still disease-ridden death traps. But they were now disease-ridden death traps that people could more or less live in, provided they watched what they drank. In 1700, average life expectancy in the West hovered around 35. By 1900, it had climbed to about 50. Not exactly paradise, but enough of an improvement that people could now live long enough to complain about it.

In short, the Industrial Revolution meant that poverty and hardship were no longer inevitable and comfort and convenience were no longer reserved for elites. They could be purchased, built and mass-produced.

And more than that, people began to suspect they should be.

The Machine Age, this is to say, didn't just change how Westerners lived; it also changed how we thought. For most of human history, there wasn't much to buy. You hunted, you foraged, you whittled something out of a stick. You skinned a woolly mammoth or made a tool from its tusks. Even in the medieval world, consumerism

116

was a rarity – shops were specialised and quite small. Serfs were subsistence farmers with simple needs and few possessions. You might treat yourself to a new jerkin if the harvest had been kind, but generally, why bother? Far better to invest in more sheep. After all, there was no social ladder to climb. If you entered a world as a serf, then a serf you would stay.

But by the 1800s, we had towns. Towns full of shops. And those shops were full of things no one had ever needed before but now absolutely had to have.

Factories revolutionised production in the 1800s, slashing labour costs and flooding markets with affordable goods. Suddenly, everyday people could afford items that had once been reserved for the upper crust. And, just like that, consumer culture was born.

In this brave new industrial world, status could be purchased. With the rise of wages, mass production and urban marketplaces, the working and middle classes were sold a new idea: you could buy your way up the ladder. You no longer needed to be defined by your lineage; you could now be defined by your stuff.

What you wore began to matter. So did what you rode, where you lived and what you arranged just-so in your parlour. For the rising middle class – factory owners, clerks, lawyers, doctors – material goods became the new language of respectability. You didn't need a title or a coat of arms. You could build your identity out of objects: a well-cut suit, a mirrored wardrobe, a piano that no one could play. You weren't who your father was. You were what your parlour looked like.

A Chesterfield armchair. A mahogany bookshelf lined with unread classics. A set of crystal glasses too delicate to ever drink out of. These possessions became personality traits. In Victorian England, etiquette manuals advised families on how to display their belongings for maximum social impact, while department stores made luxury accessible to anyone with a good hat and a bit of credit. Shopping also gave women one of their few socially acceptable freedoms – department stores became safe spaces where they could wander without a chaperone and quietly judge their neighbours' bad taste in bonnets.

The Victorians also invented the dark art of advertising. Soap wasn't just soap – it was a sign of superiority, something that would make you cleaner in both body and soul. Shopping wasn't just about owning something; it was about being someone. And once this idea caught on, there was no going back. To be fashionable meant buying, discarding, and buying again. Consumerism had found its perfect partner: insecurity. Nothing drives sales like the creeping suspicion that your neighbour's cravat looks newer.

Victorian consumerism was a fever dream of objects: mechanical egg boilers, expandable top hats, clockwork butter churns, miracle corsets, moustache protectors, tobacco tins, cravat stiffeners and decorative chamber pots. Function was optional. Symbolism was everything. A tea set was proof you were civilised. A travel case said you'd been somewhere, even if it was just to the other side of town. Families who could barely afford rent bankrupted themselves on soup spoons just to keep up appearances. If you think modern 'foodies' are pretentious, spare a thought for the Victorians, who prided themselves on owning twelve butter knives and five different forks, none of which made eating any easier.

Not everyone was impressed. Dickens mocked the age of 'facts and figures' in *Hard Times*. Thackeray skewered social climbers in *Vanity Fair*. *Punch* cartoons lampooned middle-class pretensions. And Marx fumed about 'commodity fetishism' – people worshipping objects while ignoring the sweat that it took to make them.

In 1851, Britain staged the Great Exhibition at the Crystal Palace – a vast glass greenhouse filled with sewing machines, hydraulic presses and a diamond the size of a turnip. It was consumerism turned into pilgrimage. Six million people – a third of the nation – shuffled through its glittering aisles to gape at gadgets and gewgaws. It wasn't just about industry; it was about aspiration. The Victorians weren't content to produce things; they wanted to gawp at them, worship them, and then buy smaller, cheaper versions to impress the neighbours.

These objects fed a new kind of hunger for visibility, status and that slippery thing called 'self-worth'. But is this the kind of hunger that shopping can truly satisfy? Or had we simply invented a new and stylish way to feel crap?

11

CAN'T GET YOU OUT OF MY HEAD

Why capitalism works best when you're sad

The modern advertiser does not
sell a product, but a way of life.
Vance Packard, *The Hidden Persuaders*, 1957

Karl Marx is a little out of vogue these days, despite the fact that hideous beards seem to be making a comeback. As the father of communism – i.e. a child who went a touch off the rails, what with all those gulags and purges – he's often dismissed as a source of bad ideas. But if we were to reject every creative thinker just because their creations have caused millions to suffer, most interior designers would now be in jail.

Marx, in other words, had a few valid thoughts. And, to my mind, one of his best ones was this: 'The ruling ideas of each age have ever been the ideas of its ruling class.' Culture, for Marx, wasn't just Taylor Swift or whatever crap's currently trending on TikTok. It was the story we're told – and, in time, one we tell ourselves – to justify the economic and political system we happen to be living under. Culture is a story that wraps itself neatly around the needs of that system, like a vine that's been trained to creep over the mansion of whichever rich bastard's in charge. The rulers of the day, in other words, don't just decide who gets paid. They also decide who gets praised. In any given era, the dominant worldview exists because it's a story that tells the powerless why they must remain powerless. It's a story that keeps the wheel of commerce smoothly spinning along.

Take sexism, for example, which probably dates back to the Stone Age. When your economy revolves around hunting, the people with the most strength and stamina will generally be the people who end up in charge. Which, yes, usually meant men. From the Palaeolithic age onwards, physical dominance got coded into law, lore and religion. Entire cultural structures were built to justify and maintain male power, from tribal myths to marriage contracts to burly sky gods with a penchant for rape. It's only in the last few hundred years that the economy has started to reward the ability to talk, think and type, rather than the ability to farm or hit stuff with a hammer. And because physical prowess is losing its economic usefulness, those old sexist structures are finally starting to crumble.

Or take religion, famously described by Marx as 'the opium of the people' because it functioned as a sort of anaesthetic for the horrors of feudalism – that is, a life with no wages, rights or hope. Medieval Europe's peasants didn't enjoy their suffering, but they endured it because they were told that God approved. (And why wouldn't he? Feudalism made the Church so obscenely rich, it could afford to build cathedrals the size of a shopping centre.) Not unlike the Republican party, religion helped ordinary people to make sense of their suffering while ensuring that the people on top didn't suffer at all.

But then came the Industrial Revolution. Suddenly, the big money wasn't in land, harvests or peasants; it was in machines, mines and mills. The ruling classes were no longer priests, dukes and earls; they were industrialists, bankers and railway tycoons. These people needed diligent, punctual, ambitious employees, ideally ones who would turn up six days a week, work from dawn until dusk, show lots of initiative and never ask for a pay rise. Enter the Protestant work ethic, the belief that hard work was good for your soul. In this new moral framework, being overworked and underpaid wasn't a problem; it was practically a badge of honour. Idle hands, after all, were 'the devil's playground'. Leisure was suspect, rest was laziness and fun was a slippery slope to moral decay.

The Victorians, in particular, took this philosophy to heart – and then covered it in a crisp, white tablecloth. They built entire lives around grim determination, upright postures, stiff upper lips, corsets and cold baths.

So what is the dominant culture today? I'll tell you in one word. Are you ready? Consumerism. At its core, capitalism runs on a very simple engine: supply and (yes, you guessed it) demand. Consumers demand stuff. Producers supply it. And the more stuff that's demanded, the better. Whatever it is, capitalism wants us to want it. Desperately. Endlessly. Insatiably. Interminably.

And if we don't, the machine grinds to a halt. When demand slows down, everything starts to seize up. Workers get fired. Factories shut down. Inflation rises. Share prices drop. To keep the good ship Commerce afloat, it must sail on an ocean of buyers.

All this may seem obvious now, but there was a time when it wasn't obvious at all. Right up until the early 20th century, the West still clung to a fairly strong culture of thrift. Conspicuous consumption was certainly on the rise, but it was mostly confined to the upper-middle class – that is, to those who could actually afford it. For the average working man or woman, shopping was still a largely practical affair. You bought what you needed, fixed what you had and didn't bother replacing something that still worked. No one felt compelled to own a decorative chamber pot or seventeen varieties of spats. The idea that self-indulgence was sinful – or at least a bit tacky – was deeply baked into the cultural dough.

But, by the 1920s, this sort of thinking was becoming a problem for capitalism. The issue was that, after a century or more of rapid industrialisation, most Western homes were now crammed full with stuff. With appliances. With clothes. With chairs. With cars. The basic goods that once symbolised the outer limits of prosperity had by now become fairly standard. Consumers, in short, had consumed everything they needed. And that kind of contentment was dangerous. If people stopped wanting new things, what would happen to the people who made them? What if capitalism – shock, horror – was running out of steam?

The remedy was clear: if people weren't naturally hungry for more, they would just have to be taught. If consumers didn't feel an urge to upgrade their perfectly good vacuum cleaner or toss out their sturdy old radio for a sleeker model, the solution was to stir up dissatisfaction. To make 'enough' feel like it's just not enough.

As American psychologist-turned-marketing-guru Ernest Dichter put it, 'The needs and wants of people have to be continuously stirred up.' Which is a nice way of saying: if nobody's hungry, it's time to start serving ads for imaginary meals. And so began a new era, one where satisfaction wasn't the goal but the enemy.

Enter Edward Bernays: the American nephew of Sigmund Freud and the so-called father of modern public relations. One of history's great villains, alongside Hitler and the makers of *Cats*, Bernays brought psychoanalysis to advertising. His big idea? Skip the facts and go straight for the subconscious. Target people's hidden cravings – status, love, belonging, self-worth – and they'll buy almost anything.

What if people didn't buy products for what they *did* but for how they made them *feel*? What if soap wasn't about being clean but about being attractive? What if a car wasn't for getting from A to B but for broadcasting success and impressing your friends?

As Vance Packard later put it, 'The most effective advertisements do not appeal to reason, but to the deeply buried instincts and longings within us.' Thus began the golden age of advertising, a time when companies stopped selling products and started selling *happiness*. In *The Wellness Syndrome*, sociologists Carl Cederström and André Spicer argue that the pursuit of happiness has been 'reframed as a series of consumer choices', and happiness itself has become 'a purchasable commodity'. Or, as Israeli sociologist Eva Illouz observed, we now live in a society where 'feelings have become an essential part of economic exchange'.

Every screen, every billboard began to scream the same message: happiness is just one purchase away. But if people don't feel like they're missing something, they won't spend money trying to find it. If they don't feel like they have a problem, they won't spend money trying to solve it.

Entire industries – from fashion to food to fintech – came to rely on one psychological sleight of hand: the ability to convince you that your life is missing something and they happen to sell it. The right detergent didn't just polish your sink – it polished your *reputation*. Beer didn't just quench thirst – it somehow made you a *man* (even if you happened to be a woman). Companies weren't selling soap, or cars, or breakfast cereal. They were selling *meaning*. They sold *you* – to yourself.

Throughout the 20th century, marketers perfected the art of turning objects into identities. Eventually, the shift was complete. The public had been thoroughly convinced that happiness was about *stuff.* Fulfilment, once the domain of poets and philosophers, had been hijacked by marketers. Joy could now be purchased in three easy payments.

And they made sure you never felt complete. Because in this brave new world, *enough* was never enough. Every ad, every post, every pop-up was a carefully crafted reminder that something was missing. But not to worry, for the right price, you could fill that hole.

In the early years of the Cold War, consumerism quietly became the West's favourite pastime. The economy was booming, suburbia was spreading and the threat of communism helped turn shopping into a civic duty. A house, a car, a vacuum cleaner, a colour TV – they were proof you were free, thriving and firmly on the right side of history. In short, a Western nation's greatness was measured by how many fridges its citizens could afford.

The invention of television sealed the deal. By the 1950s, advertising wasn't just in magazines or on the radio – it was beamed straight into the living room, baked into sitcoms, game shows and soap operas. Photogenic families smiled out from every screen, effortlessly content in their warm, spotless kitchens – all thanks to the right brand of cereal.

Disney, too, sold joy. Its mission – famously – was 'to make people happy'. The same logic gave us Happy Meals, Happy Hours, laugh tracks, chirpy hold music, smiley shop assistants and the eternal instruction to 'have a nice day'. Airlines painted grins on their flight attendants, toothpaste ads told you that pearly whites were the secret to popularity, and Kodak insisted that every smile be frozen forever in glossy prints. Coca-Cola told you to 'open happiness'. McDonald's announced, 'You deserve a break today.' Hallmark cards assured you that joy could be folded neatly into an envelope. Theme parks promised 'the happiest place on earth', toy companies churned out 'Fun Factories' and 'Joy Jars', and even banks got in on the act, flogging 'peace of mind' alongside their interest rates.

Increasingly, joy was encouraged and prescribed. Smiling became a kind of emotional dress code for modern life. If someone asked you how you were, the correct answer was to say you were 'good'. And if you weren't? Well, you just had to fake it – to beam in the office, grin at the shops and titter on cue during sitcoms. Not because you personally found the joke funny, but because canned laughter provided proof that it was.

By the 1980s, advertising seeped into the workplace. If consumers could be trained to seek happiness through shopping, why not employees too? A happy worker, companies reasoned, was a productive worker – and one less likely to ask for a raise. So businesses began offering happiness to their staff, along with a weekly wage. Gone were the days of punching in and zoning out. You were now expected to love your job, believe in your company's 'mission' and treat your open-plan office like a second home.

By the end of the 20th century, most Westerners had fully converted to the Gospel of Consumerism, not just through what they bought but through what they believed. Advertising had become the cornerstone of Western culture.

And in the 21st century, that gospel has only grown louder. Trillions of dollars go into ensuring we associate happiness with buying stuff. The simple joys – family dinners, leisure, a quiet Sunday afternoon – couldn't compete with the seductive promise of more. More gadgets. More outfits. More shoes. More phones. More TVs. More furniture.

More kitchen appliances. More cars. More handbags. More watches. More headphones. More books. More tools. More home décor. More gym gear. More skincare. More toys. More cleaning products. More storage containers. More everything.

And when that purchase inevitably fails to deliver lasting bliss? Not to worry, you can buy something else. And that, in a nutshell, is advertising's greatest trick. It sells a carrot that's always just out of reach. It convinces us that happiness is always just around the corner – just one more purchase away. As long as people keep chasing happiness through buying stuff, businesses will always have stuff to sell.

All in all, it's a brilliant system. Karl Marx would have been very proud.

12

I STILL HAVEN'T FOUND WHAT I'M LOOKING FOR

And why you never will

The mass of men lead lives of quiet desperation.
Henry David Thoreau, *Walden*, 1854

Full as they are of young, beautiful people seemingly in the midst of a full-body orgasm, it's tempting to think that most ads are bullshit. And it's proper and right that we do. Ecstasy is a very rare thing in this life, and it's not often found in Red Rooster.

But, in one respect, such advertisements do have a point. Whether or not owning stuff will make you beam with delight while being surrounded by a bunch of tanned hotties, it isn't all that much of a stretch to say that it's better than the alternative. Nobody daydreams about being poor. Nobody fantasises about struggling to pay rent, eating food from a tin or trying to wash socks in the sink. Surely it's not shallow, vulgar or crass to suggest it's preferable to sleep in a house rather than under a bridge, or that having a fridge and a car make life slightly more manageable. Money may not exactly buy happiness, but it makes life slightly better.

That is what common sense tells us, at any rate. And many academics seem to agree. It's a well-documented sociological truth that a certain level of material wealth correlates with a higher level of life satisfaction. Economists and psychologists have spent decades trying to measure the relationship between money and happiness. The results suggest that having enough money to cover the basics (and a little extra for treats) is one of the strongest predictors of general well-being.

Published annually since 2012, the UN's *World Happiness Report*, which ranks countries based on factors like income, social support, life expectancy and freedom, consistently sees people living in wealthier countries reporting significantly higher levels of life satisfaction than those in poorer ones. The top of the leaderboard is often dominated by the usual Scandinavian suspects – Denmark, Finland, Sweden – places where the weather sucks but education and healthcare are free.

At the individual level, the trend holds. People with sufficient income tend to report lower levels of stress, better physical health and more agency in their day-to-day lives. They're more likely to say 'yes' to a night out or leave a job that makes them weep salty tears.

But if more wealth always leads to more happiness, shouldn't we be the happiest people in history? Even the poorest Western citizens today, after all, enjoy a level of luxury and convenience that the emperors, kings and queens of old could never have dreamed of. Cleopatra may have had gold, slaves and baths full of milk and honey, but she never had noise-cancelling headphones, let alone Google Maps. Napoleon may have had hundreds of palaces, thousands of servants and the ability to sway the fate of nations with a flick of his hand, but he never got to lie on a pillowtop mattress, eat a Big Mac and say, 'Hey Siri, play Taylor Swift.' In purely material terms, modern life is a marvel. We have more disposable income, more creature comforts and more smashed avocado than any generation before us. In theory, this should make us more joyful.

But, in practice, it seems clear that we aren't. Studies show we're not actually much happier than our grandparents, despite the fact that we're better dressed, thoroughly caffeinated, comprehensively hydrated and far less likely to keel over from scurvy. The World Happiness

Report, which crunches decades of Gallup data, keeps pointing out the same awkward truth: GDP in most Western countries has soared since World War II, but average life satisfaction has basically refused to budge. Economists call this the Easterlin Paradox: money makes a difference when you don't have much of it, but once you've got Netflix, running water and a fridge that doesn't smell like death, the happiness payoff from extra cash is surprisingly small.

The 2023 Ipsos Global Advisor survey told a similar story. Polling more than 22,000 people across 32 countries, it found that in wealthy nations only about 30 per cent described themselves as 'very happy'. And that number has barely twitched in two decades, despite shinier phones, better skincare routines and more oat-milk lattes than Hesiod could ever have dreamed of. In short, modern life has fewer plagues and more playlists, but the promised 'happiness dividend' still hasn't shown up. The names change; the clothes change. The eye-rolling about life's disappointments? Eternal.

And in some cases, morale isn't just flatlining – it's getting worse and worse. According to the 2023 *Gallup Global Emotions Report*, many people across wealthy countries are experiencing unprecedented levels of sadness and stress. When asked how they felt the previous day, 42 per cent of respondents said they had experienced 'a lot' of stress, 39 per cent 'a lot' of worry and 25 per cent 'a lot' of sadness. That's not just a rough patch; that's a civilisation-wide pattern – a collective emotional downturn in countries that, economically speaking, have been on the way up.

Add rising rates of anxiety, loneliness, burnout and mental illness and it becomes clear that the material abundance of the last century isn't delivering the emotional payoff we were led to expect. Despite having more access to goods, services and protein powder than any generation before us, many people are exhausted, overwhelmed and unfulfilled. The global polling firm Gallup's CEO Jon Clifton summed it up nicely: 'We are in the midst of a global rise in unhappiness.'

So what on earth is going on here? Didn't we establish a few pages back that having more stuff tends to make people happier? Well, yes and no. As it turns out, the relationship between money and happiness doesn't come in a lovely straight line. It's more of a gentle curve that flattens into a plateau. A widely cited 2010 Princeton study by psychologist Daniel Kahneman and economist Sir Angus Deaton found that emotional well-being rises with income, but only up to around US$75,000 a year. After that, more money doesn't necessarily bring more joy, just better yoghurt and more expensive cologne. As American economist Richard Easterlin famously put it, 'There is no point of satiation in income beyond which happiness declines, but rather a plateau: more money, same mood.'

To put it simply, if you can't pay rent, money matters a lot. But if you can, it matters less than you'd think. When a person is struggling, every extra dollar can ease stress, provide some security and fund a few little joys. But after they've got the basics covered – food, a few treats, at least two pairs of undies – more money doesn't buy more happiness; it just buys more stuff. In other words, money helps until it doesn't.

This is the uncomfortable truth about consumerism. Yes, wealth can solve problems. It can fix your heater, pay for a root canal and let you order a pizza without taking out a third mortgage, but as a long-term strategy for psychological well-being, the evidence suggests it's a bit of a dud.

And if you don't believe me, just ask Abd al-Rahman III. The emir and caliph of Córdoba in 10th-century Spain, he had it all. Power, wealth, luxury. For fifty years, he reigned in peace, loved by his people, feared by his enemies and flanked by courtiers, poets and fountains. Riches and honours, he wrote, 'have waited on my call'. And yet, summing up his life at around age 70, he didn't brag about the splendour. He just did the math. 'I have diligently numbered the days of pure and genuine happiness which have fallen to my lot,' he wrote. 'They amount to 14.' Fourteen. In fifty years. That's roughly the same number of days I just spent trying to cancel my gym membership.

Or take Howard Hughes. Once the richest man in the world with yachts, planes, casinos, Hollywood studios – the works. A man so wealthy he could have bought half of Europe. And yet, he spent the final years of his life holed up in a Las Vegas hotel room, alone, naked, paranoid, refusing to cut his toenails, obsessively washing his hands and storing all his urine in jars.

And he's hardly the only one to get a little miserable. Andrew Carnegie, who made enough money in steel to buy Belgium twice, admitted, 'Millionaires who laugh are rare.' J Paul Getty installed a payphone in his mansion to stop guests from making long-distance calls, then later declared, 'I'd trade all my millions for one happy marriage.' More recently, you could ask Elon Musk, the richest man on Earth, who frequently describes his life as 'excruciating'. (Though, to be fair, I find his life excruciating too.)

Hollywood alone could fill a psychiatric hospital. Behind every red-carpet smile is a therapist's couch, a rehab stint or a prescription with a name you can't pronounce. Fame and fortune might look good on the surface, but step backstage and you'll find a thrice-divorced alcoholic drug addict weeping into their $18 juice, surrounded by awards, assistants, groupies and agents and a deep, gnawing sense they're alone.

But hang on, you say. What about retail therapy? What about the thrill of unboxing some Nike Air Jordans or strutting down the street in a pair of Christian Louboutins? Despite the fact that you're a deep thinker like me, I'm sure that you're not immune. Splurging money on overpriced crap is a widely known cure for life crises.

And it's a 'cure' that science backs up. Psychologists studying hedonic consumption have shown that buying things we *want* (as opposed to things we actually *need*) triggers a short-lived spike in dopamine, the brain's reward chemical. fMRI studies even show the pleasure centres lighting up like a Christmas tree at the mere *anticipation* of a purchase.

Problem? The effect is temporary. Morale might be lifted by a shiny new purchase, but chances are it'll sink overnight. Within a day or a week, the thrill wears off, and we're chasing the next hit – the wireless earbuds that we'll lose within minutes, or the $500 air fryer with which we'll cook frozen chips.

Like any drug, the 'retail high' fades. And once it's gone, all that's left is addiction. A constant, hollow craving for more. And an ever-deeper pit of emptiness beneath it. The richer you are, the more aware you become that other people are richer. The more stuff you have, the more stuff you realise you don't have. There is always a watch you don't have, a yacht you can't afford, a gold-encrusted doona that you just have to have. The treadmill doesn't stop – it just gets fancier. You strive, you sweat, you hustle, and just when you think you've made it, you look sideways and notice someone with more. A bigger house. A faster car.

A sommelier on staff. Chasing happiness through accumulation –
whether it's stuff, experiences, 'likes', premierships, Grammys, Oscars,
candles or cars – is like chasing the end of a rainbow. It keeps moving
away. As Alain de Botton observed, 'If status is how much you're loved
compared to how much you *want* to be loved, then consumer culture
ensures you'll always feel slightly behind.'

Want another reason why money won't make you happy for long?
It's because, at the end of the day, nothing ever will. Back in 1978,
psychologists Philip Brickman, Dan Coates and Ronnie Janoff-
Bulman from the University of Virginia ran a now-famous study
comparing two very different groups. The first was composed of people
who had just won the lottery. The second of people who had recently
been in an accident that would leave them in wheelchairs for life.
You'd expect the first group to be pretty perky and the second to feel
like shit. And for six or so months, you would have been right.

But here comes the surprise. Within a year, both groups had
returned to more or less the same levels of day-to-day happiness
and life satisfaction they had been experiencing before. Becoming
millionaires made the lottery winners happier ... for a bit. Losing the
ability to walk made the second group sadder ... for a bit. Then came
the great emotional reset.

In short, studies show that people quickly adapt to both pleasure
and pain. Psychologically speaking, we're all on a bungee cord: no
matter what happens, good or bad, we tend to return to a stable
baseline of blah. We can spring up or crash down, but eventually we
bounce back to where we started.

Big promotion? You'll be buzzing for a bit – new house, new car,
new friends – and then your inbox explodes, your calendar fills up

and you realise that your family still hates you. Get a deluxe espresso machine with twelve grind settings and a deafeningly loud milk frother? Fantastic – until you realise that it's only fucking coffee. And that most of the time, you're drinking it alone. The products vary, the branding evolves, but the emotional cycle remains consistent: novelty, joy, blah, repeat.

If the West's recent orgy of consumerism has truly changed anything, it's probably to make you feel worse. Because when you're *still* not happy, even after ticking the boxes and buying the things, you start to wonder if the problem is you.

As consumer behaviour expert Russell W Belk observed, the more we define ourselves by what we own, the more fragile our sense of self becomes. 'We live in a materialist culture,' he wrote, 'and our very identities are bound up in our possessions. But the more we are defined by what we own, the more vulnerable we are when those things fail to satisfy.' He likened the cycle of consumption to an all-you-can-eat buffet: no matter how much you consume and how ill you feel, you're tempted to go back for more.

Even those who have it all say it's not enough. As bajillionaire actor Jim Carrey remarked, 'I think everybody should get rich and famous and do everything they ever dreamed of so they can see that it's not the answer.' Trying to fill your life with possessions is like trying to fill a broken glass – it never holds. And the more you pour in, the more you will leak.

It's no wonder, then, that so many of us turn to experiences as the new holy grail of happiness. Travel. Concerts. Fancy dinners. But ultimately, the same laws apply. A 2014 study published in *Psychological Science* found that while experiences do tend to produce more lasting happiness than material goods, we still find a way to adapt to them. The trip of a lifetime eventually becomes a few blurry pics of you at the Louvre, trying to pretend that you really like art.

Happiness, in short, just can't be purchased. Wealth can remove stress, provide security and bring momentary pleasure. It can't, however, fill that hole in your soul. And thinking otherwise will just make it bigger.

13

EVERYBODY HURTS

Why having it all feels like having nothing

We live in an age in which happiness is considered
to be a right, but it is in fact a duty.
Theodore Dalrymple, *In Praise of Prejudice*, 2007

I'm sometimes told that I seem like a pretty deep thinker. (This is actually one of the few things I think deeply about.) Sure, I haven't read Sartre or an entire Russian novel, but apparently I look like I might have, probably thanks to my tendency to tune out and stare into space. Throw in my terrible dress sense and the occasional long silence, and people tend to assume there's something profound going on, when I'm really just trying hard not to fart.

But in one respect, those people aren't wrong. Moderately shallow I may well be, but I'm most certainly not materialistic. I've never believed money can buy happiness, no matter how many advertisers say otherwise. I've never imagined that everlasting joy would be mine if I just had an insanely pricey watch from Patek Philippe.

Because such people, of course, *do* actually exist – and I'm not just talking about teenage girls at Sephora. After a century of non-stop marketing, most of us know at least one or two people who truly believe that happiness can be bought. One or two people whose greatest fear isn't so much dying in a plane as having to sit in economy. I'm talking about bankers who measure success in bonuses or corporate lawyers on their third trophy wife. Then you've got Instagram influencers who are 'living the dream' or rappers who look like a jewellery store. Slightly dumber than a rock, but perhaps not quite as deep, these people's philosophy is simple: if you're not happy, you don't have enough stuff.

But here's the thing – it's not the 1980s anymore. For every vapid airhead trying to get cast in *The Bachelor*, there are at least ten vapid airheads who are sipping kombucha and talking about yoga and Zen. In the last few decades, we've seen a noticeable cultural shift away from the rampant materialism that once defined Western life and the idea that happiness is for sale.

Obviously, it all began with the Bolsheviks – and, indeed, 'lefties' of every stripe. As George Orwell famously sniffed, 'One sometimes gets the impression that the mere words 'Socialism' and 'Communism' draw towards them with magnetic force every fruit-juice drinker, nudist, sandal-wearer, sex-maniac, Quaker, 'Nature Cure' quack, pacifist and feminist in England.'

But if we can set aside the hammer and sickle, the cultural pushback against consumerism probably began with the bohemians of the 1940s– with Camus, de Beauvoir, Beckett and the like. Bohemians in black skivvies who hung out in cafes, smoked weird cigarettes and did their very best to pretend they liked jazz. In 1950s America, the Beats took up the mantle: Kerouac, Ginsberg, Burroughs and company, hitchhiking, drinking, getting high and staring into the void. Unread Dostoevsky carried for show, cigarettes smoked with studied detachment. They didn't have a lot to say but by god they said it stylishly.

Then came the 1960s, when a handful of hippies with guitars, sitars and a dislike of deodorant launched a cultural assault on the straights, stiffs and squares. Governments were corrupt. Corporations were soulless. Suburbia was a lie. Consumerism was a con. These weren't just kids skipping class to have a sneaky joint; they were kids rejecting the very foundations of Western society (and *then* having a sneaky joint). As one 1968 Gallup poll found, only 33 per cent of young Westerners said they had faith in 'the system', compared to over 70 per cent of their parents. Instead of buying cars, they bought incense. Instead of white picket fences, they sought meaning on yoga mats. Instead of dinner parties and dishwashers, they sought transcendence and dope. It was all about rejecting the plastic-wrapped joy that capitalism was selling and finding something more authentic. Something deeper. Richer. Truer. Freer. Or at least that didn't involve wearing a tie.

Of course, not all of the countercultural solutions were – how shall we put this? – airtight. Communal living sounded fun in theory, but in practice someone still had to do the washing up. LSD was not so much mind-expanding as completely life-ruining, and nobody really knew how to play a sitar. For every peaceful commune, there was a dodgy ashram run by sex pests. And if you've ever been to a week-long music festival without running water, I'm pretty sure that you no longer fear death.

Still, the central insight more or less held up throughout the 1970s: happiness wasn't entirely about Volvos or high-interest savings accounts; it was about breaking free from the grind. It was about meaning, connection and community – or at the very least owning a bean bag.

But then came the 1980s, strutting in like a stockbroker on coke, all hair gel, suspenders and shoulder pads. Ronald Reagan was in the White House. Margaret Thatcher was in Number 10 and Ayn Rand was on every bookshelf. And Satan was in every heart. Economic deregulation and global markets fuelled a decade of rampant capitalism, with luxury goods, big hair and motivational posters declaring that 'Success is a choice'. People swapped lava lamps for Motorolas the size of a brick and developed an intense emotional attachment to squash. Greed, once a sin, was rebranded as a strategy. The hippie ideals were left to gather dust beside a bong-stained shag rug.

In the space of a few years, the cultural narrative flipped. The question was no longer 'How do I escape the system?' but 'How do I win at it?' You weren't chasing enlightenment anymore – you were chasing a corner office with views.

~

But things have a way of coming back. In the first two decades of the 21st century, all that incense-scented wisdom has re-emerged. Yoga studios have sprouted up in every Western city and mindfulness apps now live in most phones. Meditation is no longer the domain of sandal-wearing mystics so much as corporate executives, and minimalism has hit the mainstream. Thanks to Japanese 'organising' consultant Marie Kondo, less is slowly becoming the new normal. People all over the West are now decluttering their homes in hopes of decluttering their minds.

Or so the theory goes. Minimalism is supposed to mean 'own less', but in practice it usually means 'buy more storage solutions'. Ancient spiritual practices designed to renounce desire now seem to require $200 yoga mats, designer leggings and a Himalayan salt lamp. What began as a path to enlightenment has been repackaged as a multi-billion-dollar industry of supplements, apps and wellness retreats where executives chant Sanskrit between PowerPoint slides. Buddha taught the end of craving; today's wellness industry teaches 'crave responsibly' – i.e. go with *vegan* bath bombs. We used to accumulate gadgets; now we collect wellness hacks. The language has changed – it's not greed, it's 'self-care' – but the pitch is the same: buy this, do this, be this, think this, and happiness will one day be yours.

In short, we're still chasing what the hippies were after – presence, peace, connection – but we're doing it in a rather natty way with lululemon and the vague, nagging sense that our inner child might also benefit from a gut detox. The countercultural ideals of the 1960s and 1970s didn't disappear. They just got sleeker branding and slightly less tie-dye.

But let's take a closer look at those 60s ideals. Because those hippies, beatniks and barefoot bohemians weren't as countercultural as they liked to think. Sure, they turned their backs on the idea that happiness could be bought with a credit card. They mocked the picket-fence life, scoffed at Tupperware parties and declared war on deodorant. But the idea that happiness was *achievable* in the first place? That part was never in doubt. In the words of American sociologist Theodore Roszak, 'To reject consumer culture was not to reject happiness – it was to reject the *fake* kind.' The counterculture didn't say, 'Stop trying to be happy.' They said, 'You're doing it *wrong*. Try *our* way instead.' So even the most 'alternative' Westerners of the past hundred years still sipped the Kool-Aid. They just chose a different flavour – kombucha instead of Coke.

If advertising has accomplished anything truly magical over the past century, it's this: it has taken a fleeting, fickle, deeply personal emotion and turned it into a formula. Not a feeling, but a finish line.

Not something you stumble into, but something you *earn*. A result. A reward. A twelve-step solution to whatever problem might ail you.

The products might vary – Nike or Adidas, wheatgrass or yoga – but the central promise remains the same: 'Happiness is yours, if only you live right.' In this worldview, joy is strategic. It's a project, a checklist, a self-improvement plan with KPIs and a digital journal. Something to monitor with your smartwatch. Something to optimise with a podcast and a probiotic.

Get fit. Eat clean. Meditate. Juice. Fast. Be grateful. Declutter your house. Ditch caffeine. Go paleo. Manifest. Read. Stretch. Buy the shoes. Take the course. Do cold plunges. Get a standing desk. Download the app. Microdose. Do breathwork. Journal. Visualise. Hike. Heal. Glow.

Do all the right things, in the right order, with the right mindset, and the universe will reward you with a shinier, more radiant version of yourself. One with glowing skin, rock-hard abs and no existential dread.

As American author Barbara Ehrenreich quipped, 'We've gone from the pursuit of happiness to the obligation of happiness.' In a world governed by marketing logic, feeling good is a *duty*. If you're not happy, you haven't bought the right supplement, found the right partner, got the right exercise regime or found the right job.

But for most of human history, happiness wasn't like this. It wasn't a project or a lifestyle – it was a fleeting accident. A rare and unexpected state of grace. A happy life was an *exceptional* life and certainly not something the average person expected to achieve between brunch and yoga class.

In medieval Europe, joy was postponed to the afterlife. Suffer now, rejoice later. In the ancient world, happiness was a gift from the gods – fragile, arbitrary, divine. The Stoics warned that chasing it was dangerous. Even the Enlightenment, the Age of Reason, with all its optimism, treated happiness as a moral and intellectual pursuit, one bound up in virtue, community and luck.

And then came advertising. And suddenly, happiness wasn't for saints, sages or philosophers anymore. It was for *everyone*. It wasn't mysterious – it was a product. Something you could get. Why wrestle with the meaning of life when you can make a protein smoothie that promises to 'revolutionise your mornings'?

And so the treadmill hums along. Always selling. Always promising. Always just out of reach. The Beats, the hippies, the wellness warriors all thought they were rejecting consumerism, but really they were just inventing shinier, more expensive versions of it. The products change – sitars, sneakers, supplements – but the promise is eternal: happiness is always just one more purchase away.

And when it doesn't arrive on time? We don't doubt or question that promise. We just question ourselves.

14

DON'T WORRY BE HAPPY

How self-help became the new scripture

Laugh and the world laughs with you.
Weep and you weep alone.
Ella Wheeler Wilcox, *Poems of Passion*, 1883

Inside every human being there lurk some deep, dark urges. To murder. To steal. To lie. To cheat. To wear socks with sandals or listen to Nickelback. But of all the crimes we are prone to, the most common is 'giving advice'. We love telling other people what they should do, what they should think, what they should say or what they should wear. If there's a human instinct stronger than self-preservation, it's the compulsion to lecture at length.

Fortunately for our ancestors, this particular impulse wasn't easy to act upon. Sure, a medieval peasant could always tell their neighbour that their pigsty was, well, a pigsty, or tell the French that they were just way too French. But they didn't have the scope to share their thoughts with the world. And even if they *did* have a self-help book rattling about inside them, the fact that the all-powerful Church claimed exclusive rights to all knowledge meant that such 'personal insights' could get you hanged.

Sadly, today's self-help writers face no such restrictions. Once upon a time, if you needed guidance, you asked your parents. Nowadays? You hop on Amazon and find thousands of titles with names like *Unfu*k Yourself, You Are a Badass, Atomic Habits, The Subtle Art of Not Giving a F*ck, 12 Rules for Life* and *Think Like a Monk*. Some books promise financial freedom. Others inner peace. A few suggest you start jogging. But whatever the particular hook might be, the message is more or less the same: happiness will be yours for the taking if you just follow the author's grand plan.

And if you don't fancy reading? Then you can download an app, enrol in a webinar or let a man with shoulder pads shout at you from a stage. There are YouTube channels, masterclasses, mindset coaches, breathwork gurus, gratitude journals, cold plunges, vision boards and dopamine detoxes. You can chant affirmations in a Mongolian yurt or align your chakras with a woman named Moonbeam. And then there are the podcasts. So many fucking podcasts. All gently implying that your entire existence would be transformed overnight if you were to just wake up early and stop eating gluten.

What began as a niche corner of the bookstore has become a full-blown subculture. You can be coached, cleansed, aligned, unblocked, biohacked, trauma-informed or spiritually activated.

The underlying pitch is as seductive as it is exhausting: you are the problem, but also the solution. Your suffering is a mindset. Your joy is a strategy. As motivational cheeseball Tony Robbins said, 'The only thing that's keeping you from getting what you want is the story you keep telling yourself.' So if you're not smashing society by Friday, that's not the system. It's all down to you.

How on earth did this shitshow begin? Well, like so much else that's wrong with the world, some of the blame surely lies with the French. Specifically, it seems to lie with Michel de Montaigne, a 16th-century French nobleman who produced thousands of pages of unsolicited advice on how best to eat, love, die, sleep and shit. 'I want death to find me planting my cabbages,' he once wrote. Everyone else wished it would find him sooner.

But the self-help industry as we know it today really began in 1859, with a book of that very name – *Self-Help* – by British government reformer Samuel Smiles. Very much a man of his age (i.e. a self-righteous prick), Smiles laid out a ruthlessly Victorian proposition: happiness was something you earned. According to Sam, if you weren't enjoying life, it wasn't due to poverty, injustice, cholera, smog or the soul-crushing futility of human existence; it was because you were slacking off. Stop waiting for God or the government to save you and get your fucking act together: 'Heaven helps those who help themselves.'

Self-Help struck a Victorian nerve. After selling over 250,000 copies in Britain alone, it became a global phenomenon, translated into multiple languages and devoured by emerging middle classes hungry for moral instruction. Smiles had created a brand, a new genre, one based on the idea that if your life wasn't going well, the problem was you. Your attitude. Your lack of effort. Your poor discipline. Your lack of character. Quite possibly, the fact that you have a weak chin and, if we're honest, you smell. Happiness, success and fulfilment were all within reach; you just had to reach out and grab them.

Once people realised they could make a fortune telling other people this shit, the self-help floodgates burst open. What began as fringe enthusiasm quickly became a cultural mainstay. Self-help books marched proudly from the margins of polite conversation to centre stage.

And marching in lockstep, right beside them? Pseudoscientists, in crisp white lab coats. The early 20th century gave us cars, radios, telephones and motion pictures. The spirit of the age was one of rational control and mechanical mastery. Cities were being electrified, workers were timed with stopwatches and every social ill seemed fixable with the right spreadsheet. This was the golden age of invention.

But it was also the golden age of absolute horseshit. It was an age that sold phrenology kits and vibrating belts for 'spot fat reduction'. An age in which people drank radioactive water for 'vitality'. You could buy electric hairbrushes that claimed to cure baldness and foot-operated machines that promised to jiggle the depression right out of you. Auras could be photographed. Futures could be divined. Personality types were determined by bumps on your head.

Naturally, happiness didn't escape the same treatment. What had once been a slow, messy, philosophical pursuit – a question agonised over by homosexual poets and bearded weirdos in togas – was now repackaged as a proto-scientific discipline. Self-help writers tapped into the hopeful logic of the modern age: that everything – even joy – could be learned, mastered and systematised. There were acronyms. There were charts. There were programs and formulas. Happiness came with deadlines, diagrams and motivational homework.

By the 1920s, books promising 'scientific' solutions to personal problems were flooding the market. There were titles like Dale Carnegie's 1936 self-help book, one of the bestselling books of all time, *How to Win Friends and Influence People*, as well as *The Power of Thought* and *Your Mind and How to Use It*. They promised firmer handshakes, whiter teeth, stronger jawlines and better lives. If you just repeated the right affirmation, practised the right posture, or stood in front of a mirror with enough confidence, the universe would eventually reward you.

One of the most popular titles was by British psychiatrist Harold Dearden. His 1926 book *Understanding Ourselves: The Fine Art of*

Happiness told readers they could engineer their own well-being. Mood, Dearden argued, was a mechanical issue. If you could train your brain properly through willpower, clean thoughts and plenty of cornflakes, happiness would roll off the conveyor belt.

Then came World War II. Cities were reduced to rubble. Economies burst into flames. People had seen things – horrible things. They needed a reason to believe in any old shit.

And any old shit was just what they got.

In 1952, *The Power of Positive Thinking*, by Norman Vincent Peale, offered the kind of fatuous optimism the postwar West was craving. His pitch? Positive thinking could rewire your life. 'Change your thoughts and you change your world.' If you see the glass as half-full, not half-empty, in time it will become a solid gold goblet lavishly encrusted in diamonds and rubies and overflowing with Dom Pérignon. Once described by Donald Trump as 'the greatest book ever written', *The Power of Positive Thinking* quickly flew off the shelves.

By the 1960s and 1970s, the tone of self-help slightly shifted. Out went hard work and in came introspection. Happiness was about finding yourself. Self-help merged with pop psychology to produce mega-sellers like *I'm OK – You're OK*, which introduced millions to the idea that their adult problems could be blamed on their parents. The stiff upper lip was replaced by the trembling lower one, and suddenly, every second person was 'processing' their childhood.

Then came the 1980s, when self-help got all Gordon Gekko. In swaggered motivational speaker Tony Robbins with *Awaken the Giant Within*, a book that made yelling at yourself in the mirror feel like a legitimate life strategy. A 24-carat cheese-ball with hair gel and shoulder pads, Robbins' gospel was simple: summon your 'peak state', man the fuck up and grab hold of life like she's a hot, busty blonde. Meanwhile, corporate bookshelves groaned under the weight of *Who Moved My Cheese?*, *The Seven Habits of Highly Effective People* and *Feel the Fear and Do It Anyway*.

By the 1990s and early 2000s, self-help had become an unstoppable cultural juggernaut. Oprah built an empire on it, turning books like *The Road Less Travelled*, *A New Earth* and *You Can Heal Your Life* into staples of daytime TV. 'Living your best life' became a popular phrase and 'life coach' a common profession.

Then came *The Secret*, a film and book combo that promised you a way to manifest your dreams. (Just think hard enough about what you want and the universe will deliver it. There, I saved you from having to read it.)

And that, more or less, brings us to now, where self-help has gone fully digital. We're living in the age of podcasts, TikTok gurus, 'mindset hacks', and an endless scroll of twerps telling us to eat more protein. The self-help industry keeps on keeping on, and there's no reason to believe it will ever stop. After all, it sells a dream. A shiny, flickable, clickable dream, where everything you want is always just within reach.

But the real genius is that it's only a dream. If self-help actually helped anyone, the market would promptly collapse. But instead of delivering fulfilment, it dangles new problems and shinier solutions just out of reach – like a treadmill made of buzzwords. Sick of chasing *happiness*? That's fine. Try *resilience*. Or *productivity*. Or *emotional intelligence*. Or *grit*. Or *flow*. Or *mindfulness*. Or an *abundance mindset*. Or *purpose*. Or *clarity*. Or *alignment*.

Like pretty much every Coldplay song, all these supposedly unique goals are variations on the same theme. They're just new ways to describe the same basic longing – the longing to feel better, to be better, to finally *arrive*. To live and breathe in some magical state where everything makes sense and nothing hurts. Whether you call it contentment, calm, confidence, inner peace, peak performance or radical self-love, the underlying promise is always happiness.

And, of course, it's always just out of reach. There's always one more tweak. One more acronym. One more book. One more guru who's finally cracked the code your last five gurus mysteriously missed. As the journalist Barbara Ehrenreich quipped, 'Personal development is a never-ending to-do list.'

Self-help has come a long way since Samuel Smiles, but the basic message has remained the same. If you're not feeling good, it's probably your fault. Bottom line: you are doing life wrong.

15

MAD WORLD

When misery became mental illness

I do not believe anyone can be perfectly
well, who has a brain and a heart.
Henry Wadsworth Longfellow,
The Letters of Henry Wadsworth Longfellow, 1967

It's often said that the times maketh the man, and like most clichés it's often quite true. Steve Jobs couldn't have invented the iPad before we discovered electricity. Shakespeare might have struggled in an age without ink. And if Donald Trump had run for president before Fox News came along, I'm pretty sure he'd now be in jail.

Which brings us to Sigmund Freud, a cocaine-addled psychoanalyst with a penis fixation and some slightly unsettling theories about me and my mum. Drop Sigmund into the medieval era and he wouldn't be inventing psychiatry – he'd be diagnosing demons and trialling cures for the 'possessed'. Ranging from leeches and lobotomies to prayers and chains, treatment for mental illness used to be as helpful as Qantas's customer service.

But Freud was born in turn-of-the-century Vienna, a city buzzing with cafes, salons, bohemian angst and people just dying to talk about their dreams. He arrived at a cultural sweet spot, a moment when Western society was finally open to the radical idea that the human mind was a thing worth investigating. The couch, the confession, the dream journal – all of it only works in a culture newly obsessed with looking inward and ready to believe that talking about yourself isn't indulgent or insane ... but science.

So, what did Freud actually say? In short, most of your problems can be traced back to your childhood and/or some repressed desire you don't want to admit to. And these problems, he argued, could be unearthed through talking, ideally while lying on a brown leather couch. His ideas were equal parts genius and coco bananas, but they did give birth to a new science: psychiatry.

But as psychiatrists themselves remind us, kids don't always grow up the way their parents imagined. Would the father of the discipline even recognise his child today? What would Freud make of the 21st-century mental health industry, an industry that more or less treats unhappiness as an illness to be diagnosed? Without wanting to sound like the kind of pathetic old man who calls up talkback radio to complain about 'snowflakes', it sometimes feels like we're living in an era where every personality trait or emotional wobble seems to come with a label or pill. Feeling sad? Could be depression. A bit nervous before a presentation? Might be generalised anxiety. Trouble concentrating at work? Could be ADHD. Don't like parties? Maybe it's social anxiety. Tired all the time? Could be trauma. Can't stand your job? Might be a toxic workplace. Get bored in relationships? Possibly avoidant attachment. Struggle with anger? Maybe you're neurodivergent. Struggle to get out of bed on Mondays? Could be seasonal affective disorder or your circadian rhythms.

Obviously, I exaggerate. But it's not an exaggeration to say that Freud would have raised an eyebrow at all of this (unless he was busy thinking about penises). He believed, quite sensibly, that a bit of suffering was normal. Life, in his view, was never meant to be a non-stop parade of joy. In his 1920 essay *Beyond the Pleasure Principle*, he wrote that the best therapy could offer was to replace 'hysterical misery with ordinary unhappiness'. He didn't promise beaming, well-adjusted optimists. He promised functionality. One of his core ideas was the repetition compulsion, the brain's strange habit of revisiting trauma in an attempt to make sense of it. The goal of therapy was to stop the pain from taking over. It was all about damage control.

But, as sales pitches go, this wasn't so great. Therapy, as Freud described it, sounded less like a spa day for the soul and more like a psychological war of attrition. It involved years of analysis, endless talk about your upbringing and the slow excavation of trauma. It wasn't exactly what you'd call fun. So in the 1930s and 1940s, a new wave of psychologists began pushing back against the gloom. Thinkers like Carl Rogers and Abraham Maslow suggested that psychology shouldn't just study what makes people miserable; it should study what helps them flourish.

But the real game changer in the happiness-industrial complex might have been pharmaceuticals. Sure, humans have been self-medicating for millennia. The ancient Sumerians even called opium the 'joy plant'. But the modern, chemical pursuit of happiness didn't truly kick off until the 20th century. In 1937, American pharmaceutical company Smith, Kline & French released Benzedrine, a nasal decongestant packed with amphetamine. It wasn't long before people realised that its side effects included feeling *terrific*. Marketed as 'pep in a pill', it was soon repurposed for anything that didn't respond to caffeine: fatigue, mild depression, low motivation, a slight disclination to wash your socks. Housewives took it to vacuum. Students popped it to cram. Executives took it to dominate the boardroom. *The Los Angeles Times* called it 'a miracle compound for modern life'.

As the pharmaceutical industry exploded, so did the idea that every emotional or mental hiccup could be – and should be – chemically solved. Pills were no longer just for pain or infection; they were for personality.

And so began a long, lucrative partnership between mental health and medication, one in which 'feeling better' meant finding the right prescription. Barbiturates for nerves. Stimulants for sluggishness. Sedatives for grief. If Freud offered decades of analysis, drug companies offered a pill and a pamphlet.

Then came the blockbusters. In 1987, Prozac hit the market and racked up 2.5 million prescriptions in under a year. Ritalin became the classroom cure for daydreaming. Xanax soothed anxiety like a chemical cup of tea.

What had once been a philosophical quest to understand the soul's sorrows was outsourced to neurotransmitters and synapses. As American comedian Marc Maron once put it, 'I used to think my brain was just naturally like this. Turns out it was just low serotonin.'

And as the number of mental health diagnoses has grown, so too has the number of patients.

As the World Health Organization noted in 2022, 'Globally, mental health conditions are on the rise.' According to a 2022 issue of *The Economist*, 'Mental illness now accounts for a third of all disability claims in the West. In some countries, it is now the leading cause of disability.' Emergency rooms are seeing record numbers of psychiatric admissions, antidepressant prescriptions are at all-time highs and anxiety disorders are now among the most common medical conditions in developed countries.

So what the hell is going on here? Has Western life truly become that unbearable? Some say yes and argue that we're in the midst of a genuine mental health crisis, fuelled by climate anxiety, financial instability, loneliness and ubiquitous screens. Personally, I'd still rather be alive now. Life expectancy is up. Poverty is down. McDonald's special meal deals are just $6.95. In all sorts of ways, life has never been better.

A more likely explanation, in my mind, for the apparent explosion of mental illness is that people are better at talking about it. American psychologist Jean Twenge suggests that increased diagnoses may reflect an increased level of awareness, not necessarily a surge in pathology. 'More people are identifying and treating mental health issues that were once ignored,' she writes. In the past, you were told to 'toughen up'. Now, you're told to 'talk it out'. And, of course, that's a good thing.

But it also raises a very good question. Where do we and should we draw the line between genuine mental illness and ordinary human misery? After all, doctors have never been shy about overservicing. From boiled toads to bloodlettings to opium sleep aids for kids, the medical profession has historically shown itself more than happy to treat ordinary discomfort as some kind of crisis.

In the 2007 book *The Loss of Sadness*, American sociologists Allan Horwitz and Jerome Wakefield tackle this precise topic. They argue that modern psychiatry has stretched the definition of mental illness so far that everyday emotional pain – the kind that comes with breakups, burnout or bad bosses – now qualifies as clinical pathology. 'The boundaries between normal distress and disorder,' they write, 'have become so porous that everyday emotions are increasingly being labelled as mental illnesses.'

Barbara Ehrenreich made a similar point but with a bit more bite: 'The more we come to understand mental illness, the more we seem to suffer from it.'

Psychologist Jonathan Haidt issued a stark warning in 2023: 'We have raised a generation in a culture of fragility and we are now seeing the psychological bill come due.' In other words, we may not be suffering more than past generations. We may simply be expecting it less. It may be that when life fails to be flawless, we treat that failure as a crisis. We diagnose ourselves. We pathologise what it is to be human.

None of this is to suggest that mental illness isn't real. It absolutely is. Depression, anxiety, PTSD, bipolar disorder – these are not moods or phases. They are serious, often life-altering experiences that demand serious treatment. You can't walk off a panic attack. You can't gratitude-journal your way out of trauma. And you certainly can't hug away schizophrenia.

But we have created a culture in which happiness is an expectation and sadness, stress or uncertainty are no longer seen as part of being human but as signs that something has gone wrong. We believe every mind should function like a new iPhone: smooth, efficient and glitch-free.

And that's a big problem, because life will always be hard. Suffering isn't a flaw to be fixed. Feeling anxious is not a malfunction. Sometimes, a cigar is just a cigar. And a bad day is just a bad day.

16

UNDER PRESSURE

*Why we're better off than ever –
and somehow feeling worse*

Life is full of misery, loneliness and
suffering – and it's all over much too soon.
Woody Allen, *Love and Death*, 1975

So here we are, folks. Roughly 300,000 years since Homo sapiens first came into being and figured out how to farm. From stone tools to smoothies, we've created all sorts of stuff to make our lives better. And, by and large, they have worked very well.

We're richer, safer, healthier and better educated than any generation in history. We have more comfort, more choice, more support and more skincare. What once would've killed a Roman emperor can now be fixed with nothing more than a bandaid. Inventions that would once have dazzled a nation are now par for the course. We've got sushi on demand, wi-fi in our pockets, pillows made of latex and cars that park themselves. Hairdressers, therapists, dieticians, chiropractors and personal trainers are all just a few clicks away. We can send memes across continents. We have apps that can diagnose a rash. We have climate-controlled homes, robot vacuums, smart lighting and ergonomic chairs. We have central heating, video calls, healthcare, democracy, vaccines, Spotify, electric toothbrushes, pizza ovens and hair gel. Mental health is now part of the public conversation and squadrons of professionals are on hand to advise on it. And if you're female, black, gay, trans or disabled, there has never been a better time to be alive.

Of course, society could still be better. Inequality persists. Injustice lingers. The environment's fucked and Donald Trump is still in power.

But by most reasonable measures, most of us have never had more reasons to feel content. We've never had more freedom to pursue happiness, or more information about what it involves. So you would think that our pursuit of happiness must be going pretty well.

And yet, you'd be wrong. We are, somehow, more miserable than ever. What's emerging across continents and class lines is what many are now calling a full-blown mental health pandemic. Pretty much every major study from the past few decades confirms the same bleak trend: life satisfaction is falling and rates of loneliness, anxiety, depression and addiction are all starting to soar.

Between 1990 and 2019, the number of people suffering from anxiety disorders climbed from 195 million to 301 million, while depression rose from 182 million to 290 million. That's nearly 600 million people now living with daily psychological distress. The numbers only get darker from there: more than 700,000 people die by suicide every year – roughly one every 40 seconds. 'Mental health is a growing crisis,' the World Health Organization warned in 2022, 'and one of the leading causes of disability worldwide.' All over the Western world and beyond, people are increasingly unhappy, unsettled and unsure whether things will get better.

In the United States, the picture is especially alarming. The percentage of adults diagnosed with depression more than doubled between 1990 and 2017, rising from 3.3 per cent to 7.1 per cent. By 2023, Gallup reported that nearly one in five adults had been diagnosed with depression – the highest rate ever recorded. 'America is facing an unprecedented mental health crisis,' declared US Surgeon General Vivek Murthy in 2021. 'This crisis is the defining public health challenge of our time.'

Among younger Americans, the statistics are even more troubling. In 2023, a Centers for Disease Control and Prevention report found that 57 per cent of teenage girls reported persistent feelings of sadness or hopelessness – up from just 28 per cent in 2011. Nearly 30 per cent had seriously considered suicide.

University students aren't doing much better. A Harvard study tracking undergraduates from 2014 to 2018 found that depression rose from 22 per cent to 31 per cent, while anxiety jumped from 19 per cent to 30 per cent. And in 2022, the American College Health Association found that 77 per cent of students reported moderate to serious psychological distress. As the *Chronicle of Higher Education* observed, 'College mental health services are overwhelmed and students are struggling.'

The UK, too, is on a downward slope. According to the Office for National Statistics, self-reported happiness and life satisfaction have stagnated or declined steadily since 2011. And in a 2023 Gallup poll, only 44 per cent of Americans described themselves as 'very satisfied' with their personal lives – the lowest figure in over 20 years. The 2023 Gallup *Global Emotions Report* also recorded a global uptick in stress, sadness and worry, with 2022 ranking as 'the most negative year on record since we began tracking emotional states in 2006'.

Meanwhile, the safer we get, the more unsafe we all seem to feel. Child mortality has collapsed, crime has tanked, medicine actually works – and yet parents now hover like helicopters, convinced every sandpit hides a used syringe. The modern West is statistically safer than any era in history, but also drowning in warnings, disclaimers and helmet laws. Our ancestors wrestled bears, crossed oceans and sent kids up chimneys; we panic about gluten, excessive screen time and whether or not trampolines have a safety net.

And none of this is helped by the relentless forebodings of doom pumped out by the 24-hour news cycle. In earlier centuries, you might have worried about the harvest or the next invasion; today you wake up fretting about trade wars, interest rates and climate collapse before you've had your morning coffee. As Neil Postman warned, the news industry is designed less to inform than to keep us 'in a continual state of anxiety, panic, and amusement'.

Meanwhile, Australia – the land of sunshine and surf – is quietly enduring its own slow-motion mental health crisis. According to Beyond Blue, over two million Australian adults are living with anxiety, while roughly one in seven experience depression in any given year. In 2022 alone, 3249 Australians died by suicide – more than three times the national road toll. 'This is not just a crisis of individuals,' said Beyond Blue CEO Georgie Harman, 'it's a national emergency.' In 2022, the Australian Bureau of Statistics reported that more than a third of the population now lives with a mental or behavioural condition.

Young Australians, in particular, are doing it tough. The 2023 *Mission Australia Youth Survey*, which gathered responses from over 19,000 young people aged 15 to 19, found that mental health was named the number one issue facing the nation – for the fifth year in a row. More than one in three said they were personally 'very concerned' about their own mental well-being.

National well-being data backs up this sense of unease. According to the 2023 *Australian Unity Wellbeing Index*, overall life satisfaction had dropped to its lowest level in the survey's 24-year history – lower than during the Global Financial Crisis, the COVID lockdowns and the year Scott Morrison became prime minister.

Meanwhile, anxiety is in its golden age. A 2023 UNICEF report found that one in five adolescents worldwide now suffers from a mental health condition, with anxiety and depression leading the charge. The same report warned that untreated mental illness remains 'one of the most neglected issues in global health'.

So here we are, living at a time when things have never been better. And yet somehow we feel worse and worse. The richest, safest, most comfortable people in human history – lying awake night after night, consumed with stress, fear and dread.

Which leaves us with the uncomfortable question: if modern life is so good, why do we feel so bad?

17

(I CAN'T GET NO) SATISFACTION

Why chasing joy makes us miserable

The difference between what we expect from life and
what life actually delivers is the cause of most unhappiness.
Alain de Botton, *The Course of Love*, 2016

So what the hell's going on here? Why, in an age of unprecedented comfort, security and self-actualisation, are so many of us so very sad?

Well, I have a thought. And given that we're now on chapter 17, it's probably about time that I got to it. Maybe the problem is *not* how we feel. Maybe the problem is with how we think we *should* feel. Most of us, I'd suggest, are probably about as happy as we can be, all else being equal in the general scheme of events. The problem is that we're rarely, if ever, as happy as we think we *ought* to be. And that gap – between what we experience and what we expect – is, by and large, making us miserable.

What, precisely, do I mean by this? It's a good question; I'm glad that I asked. Have you ever noticed the strange power of false expectations? How the movie everyone insists is 'life-changing cinema' is almost always a tedious letdown? Or how a $120 bottle of Château d'Yquem, 'with fragrant white flower accents, lingering chalk nuances and fruity aromas of Mirabelle plum and fresh apricot', often ends up tasting a whole lot like wine?

It's the anticipation that does it. When we're told something will be amazing, our brains start pre-loading the dopamine. But when reality shows up with something that's merely *fine*, that dopamine fizzles. And we don't just feel neutral. We feel disappointed. Sometimes even defective.

Excessive expectations raise the bar and handcuff us to it. A $6 pinot from Aldi can taste brilliant because we expect donkey piss. A film that scored 10 per cent on Rotten Tomatoes might surprise and delight. The same principle applies to holidays, restaurants, dates, careers, concerts and TV shows that, at first glance, look crap.

The tragedy is, the thing itself hasn't changed. The movie is the same. The wine is the same. What's changed is the expectation we brought to the table. Welcome to the quiet tyranny of expectation, a ruthless regime that ruins perfectly good things simply because they're not 100 per cent perfect.

And, like all good tyrants, it can ruin your life. If you expect your work to be filled with passion, purpose, meaning and zest, even a great job will feel like a grind. If you expect your partner to be your soulmate, your therapist and your personal sex wizard, then even a healthy, loving relationship will feel like a letdown. When we expect every element of our lives – our careers, our couches, our dinner parties – to deliver transcendent joy, we make it impossible for *enough* to ever feel like … enough.

The ordinary becomes unacceptable. The adequate feels inadequate. And happiness, once it's expected to be constant, starts to vanish altogether. The same phenomenon applies to life itself. Most of the time, the problem isn't that life is bad. It's that we expect it to be amazing – all the time. And when it's not, we assume something must be broken. The job. The relationship. Us.

Weddings are the classic example. They're hyped as the 'best day of your life', complete with $10,000 dresses and speeches that go on longer than Tolstoy and may as well have been written in Russian. Then the cake tastes like cardboard and Uncle Darren gets drunk and sings

Cold Chisel. The problem isn't the wedding – it's the expectation that one day should be transcendent enough to justify a second mortgage.

But it's not just weddings and parties; it can be anything. Real life can never compete with the fantasies we construct for it. Because life is, well, life – it stumbles, it plateaus, it forgets to buy the milk. But instead of accepting that, we compare it to an imagined ideal: a highlight reel of how things *should* feel. So when work feels a little boring, we don't shrug and move on – we panic and assume we've taken a wrong turn somewhere.

The issue isn't that our lives are terrible. It's that we've decided they must be extraordinary. All the time. In every way. 'Good' no longer feels good enough. 'Enjoyable' barely registers. 'Comfortable' feels like settling. The more we demand that every moment be incredible, the harder it becomes to appreciate anything that's merely ... nice.

Once upon a time, people were thrilled just to reach adulthood with all their limbs intact. Simply surviving was cause for celebration. These days, survival doesn't cut it. You can have a stable job, a kind partner, a roof over your head and a few close friends – and still feel like a failure because your abs aren't visible and your podcast only has four listeners.

We've set the bar so high that nothing clears it. We chase perfection so relentlessly that even success feels like disappointment. Got a promotion? Great – what are they paying you? Ran a marathon? Fantastic – shame about your time. Cooked a beautiful meal? Congrats – too bad about the photo.

But the real damage isn't just to our expectations of life; it's to our expectations of ourselves. It's no longer enough to be successful, healthy or even fulfilled. Now we're expected to *feel* amazing about it – constantly. To glow with joy. To radiate gratitude, purpose and inner peace, 24/7.

Just as no one wants to be seen as poor or unkempt, we now live in a culture where emotional discomfort carries its own quiet shame. Sadness, boredom, anxiety or frustration aren't just unpleasant – they're suspicious. A sign that something's gone wrong. That *you've* gone wrong. If you're not leaping out of bed with a smile, seizing the day and inhaling rose-scented mindfulness, the message is clear: you're failing. (And probably also letting down those fine folks at the gym.)

Everywhere we look – in ads, apps, corporate slogans and Instagram captions – we're told that unhappiness is unacceptable. And this is where the pressure really kicks in. Because when we *don't* feel great, we judge ourselves for it. We pathologise it. Instead of accepting sadness or stress as part of being human, we treat them like malfunctions. We feel bad ... and then we feel bad about feeling bad.

Psychologists June Gruber, Iris Mauss and Maya Tamir call this spiral meta-unhappiness, the experience of not just suffering, but suffering *wrong*. You're sad, then ashamed of being sad, then anxious that you're not snapping out of it fast enough. As they put it, 'We don't just suffer – we suffer wrong.' In today's culture, sadness is a failure.

A few hundred years ago, people didn't think this way. Emotions were like weather – inconvenient, unpredictable, but expected. You didn't track them, optimise them or explain them in therapy-ready language. You didn't ask whether your melancholy was 'helping you grow'. You just felt it – and got on with your day.

Today, that's no longer allowed. We want to feel *amazing* all the time. Fear, envy and grief aren't just difficult emotions anymore.

They're evidence you've failed at life. And instead of simply experiencing them, we interrogate them, analyse them, try to hack them into submission.

Instead of letting ourselves be sad or scared or exhausted, we scold ourselves for it. Instead of suffering from deprivation, we suffer from expectation – and the belief that our lives should *never* feel broken. The problem isn't that life is bad; it's that life is fine – and fine now feels like failure. The tyranny of expectation isn't that we don't get what we want. It's that we expect too much to begin with.

18

9 TO 5

Why work is so much work

We have created a society based on the idea that work is not just a means of earning a living or a social obligation but the very purpose of life.
David Graeber, *Bullshit Jobs: A Theory*, 2018

Absent-minded waiter. Perpetually late babysitter. Permanently stoned stock taker. Deeply shit chef. I've had some pretty bad jobs in my time and, in turn, done them all pretty badly. But as much as I (and my customers) hated my time in the kitchen, it's probably fair to say that plenty of workers have had it far worse. For most of history, what we'd now call 'the job market' might have been described by a neoliberal economist as 'a dynamic system of flexible labour arrangements'. In other words, a treadmill powered by the bones, blood and sweat of the poor.

The Middle Ages, for example, may have featured knights, dukes and earls, but such jobs were the exception, not the rule. Far more common were the peasants, street rats, guttersnipes and riffraff who spent their days in cesspits, coalmines and sewers. Slaughtering sheep. Skinning cows. Sweeping chimneys. Shovelling poo. Catching rats was also a popular career option unless you preferred being killed in some long, pointless war. 'The lives of the poor were a ceaseless round of toil and hunger, filth and fear,' is how Barbara Tuchman puts it – and life didn't seem to get much better in the years after that. The Industrial Revolution basically invented the modern concept of being worked to the bone, while you slowly died from a case of black lung. Think sixteen-hour shifts, six days a week, in windowless firetraps filled with poisonous fumes, deafening machines, asbestos and a thick haze of soot. Wages were pitiful, breaks were rare, injuries were common and sudden death not unknown. The term 'work–life balance' did not exist, and 'health and safety' was just a waste of good coal. You could be fired for being late, falling ill or coughing up blood on the boss's clean floor.

And children, of course, were right in the thick of it, because what better way to spend the precious years of youth than squeezing up a chimney, down a mine or between the long, sharp blades of some dodgy machine? In 1842, the British Mines Commission found children as young as 5 were working underground for up to twelve hours a day. Kids lost fingers, arms and, quite often, their lives. But that was okay, because their lives were quite shit. As Charles Dickens wrote of one child labourer, 'He ate the bread of sorrow and drank the tears of industry.'

Meanwhile, for a huge number of women, your career options were basically 'maid' or 'prostitute', though the line between them could often get rather blurry. As Judith Walkowitz notes, 'prostitution was not a marginal occupation – it was a central part of the urban economy, fuelled by poverty, shaped by gender inequality and policed through shame'. And even the jobs deemed 'respectable' were rarely much chop. Needlewomen stitched until their fingers bled, while laundresses worked ankle-deep in freezing water laced with lye, scrubbing clothes for fourteen hours a day.

But even though such men, women and children did it tough, in one sense they were the lucky ones because they actually got paid. However grim the job, however foul the air, however ugly the customer or soul-crushing the hours, all such employees would eventually get a few coins. Or maybe a hunk of bread or a few swigs of gin. Basically, just enough not to die. But not quite enough to stop wishing you would.

Now imagine being one of the workers who didn't even get that – one of the people who weren't people but *property*. In ancient Rome, it's estimated that slaves made up as much as 40 per cent of the population. They were everywhere – in fields, mines, kitchens, brothels, galleys and amphitheatres. In some regions, they outnumbered citizens two to one. Bought, sold, branded and whipped, they farmed crops, rowed ships, laid aqueducts and hauled marble. Some were forced into prostitution. Others were mauled by animals for public amusement.

In the American South, meanwhile, millions of men, women and children spent the 19th century toiling in cotton fields, sugar plantations, tobacco farms and early factories. They were beaten, starved, shackled, raped and frequently separated from their children or spouses. The transatlantic slave trade alone transported over twelve million Africans into bondage, with at least 1.8 million dying during the voyage, their corpses dumped in the sea. American historian Marcus Rediker called the Atlantic 'the largest unmarked graveyard in the world'.

And this wasn't confined to the Americas. Slavery was practised in ancient Greece, Egypt, China, India, the Islamic caliphates, the Ottoman Empire and across pre-modern Europe and Africa. Aristotle casually described slaves as 'living tools'. In Ottoman harems, women were imprisoned, silenced and traded like livestock. In the Belgian Congo, less than 150 years ago, workers had their hands hacked off if they failed to meet rubber quotas. Even neoliberal economists might draw the line at that bold new model of incentivised performance management, even though it was clearly brimming with entrepreneurial spirit.

So, yes, my cooking skills were suboptimal. But no one beat me for it, as much as they might have wanted to. No one sold my children, fed me to a lion or chained me to a tree as they whipped flesh from my bones. When we bang on today about how much work sucks, it's a contrast worth keeping in mind.

Now, credit where it's due. A lot of those ye olde jobs did have a few perks. I mean, by and large, people got plenty of exercise. They never had to navigate Microsoft Teams, chat with Kevin from Accounts or hear someone say, 'Let's put a pin in that.'

But let's not get carried away. The truth is, after more than 200 years of unions and labour reform, we in the West have mostly clawed our way out of the worst form of exploitation (or at least outsourced it to sweatshops in Asia). The horrors of slavery, soot-choked factories and eighteen-hour shifts are mostly behind us (or, rather, far away in the East). These days, 'hard labour' refers to a particularly annoying spreadsheet or a strategy meeting that lasts more than an hour. We're unlikely to get cholera from the office water cooler, and the worst physical injury most of us will suffer at work is a sore foot from kicking a printer. You are statistically unlikely to be attacked by a wolf, and your boss probably won't have you executed for a typo. And unless you work in a corporate law firm, you're also not spending your days knee deep in shits.

So next time you're talking about quarterly projections, or pretending to care that it's Kevin's birthday, it's worth remembering you're living in a workers' paradise. There are snacks in the common room, coffee in a pot, chairs that roll, casual Fridays and sick leave. The air is temperature-controlled and you'll be home before 10. Work, on the whole, has never been more comfortable. In short, we should be counting our blessings. We've never had it so good.

But are we counting our blessings? No, we're not. By and large, we all think we're in hell. The modern office worker has better conditions than 99 per cent of people in history, and yet stress and dissatisfaction are at record highs. According to the World Health Organization, workers have never been more burned out, exhausted or existentially drained. Burnout, characterised by three key symptoms – chronic exhaustion, rising cynicism and a growing sense that nothing you do matters – is sweeping through Western civilisation like an emotional bushfire.

A 2021 Gallup poll found that 76 per cent of employees experience burnout at least sometimes, with 28 per cent saying they feel it 'often' or 'always'. That's nearly a third of the global workforce who, despite being safe, heated and ergonomically seated, feel like their soul is slowly turning to dust.

In Australia, a 2023 survey by SuperFriend, *Indicators of a Thriving Workplace*, suggests that 42 per cent of all workers experience symptoms of burnout. That's nearly half the workforce fighting mental fatigue while trying to remember their wi-fi password. Safe Work Australia reports that almost one in ten serious workers' compensation claims now cite mental health conditions such as stress, anxiety and depression. And a 2022 Beyond Blue study found that one in five Australian workers had taken time off due to mental health struggles.

The Protestant work ethic, meanwhile, is losing its shine. More and more people want to work less and less. A 2023 Australia Institute poll found that over 80 per cent of Australians support a four-day workweek. Gone are the 1980s fantasies of corner offices, constant air travel, shoulder pads and making deals over steaks. These days, most of us would settle for more free time so we can spend it having a cry in the car park.

So what on earth is going on here? Once again, I suspect it all comes down to expectations. Modern Western culture has given work a role in our lives that it was never meant to fulfil. More and more people feel like they're failing at their careers because they've been set up to expect the impossible. In this case, the expectation is that 'the right job' will make them happy.

As David Graeber observed in *Bullshit Jobs*, the very idea that we should like our work is 'a peculiar anomaly in human history'. For most of the past, work wasn't supposed to fulfil you; it was supposed to feed you. Obeying your lord or whomever was a means to an end: a way to keep the fire burning, some straw over your head and a wooden spoon with which to eat your pottage. You did it, you got paid and then you went home and complained. Your employer gave you a wage and, in return, you gave them forty years of your life and a gradually deteriorating spine. If you were lucky, you'd retire with a gold watch.

And if you happened to enjoy your career, well, that was a happy accident, like finding a real estate agent who isn't a twat. If you didn't, there were always pubs, hobbies, football or the weekend. Long story short: you didn't have to love your job. You just had to go out and do it.

This was a time when your job didn't define you, when no one asked 'What do you do?' because they thought the answer would reveal who you were. Once upon a distant time, no one expected your career to reflect your personality. You could be a butcher from 9 to 5 and still be a father, a friend, a poet, a dreamer, a fisherman and a fan of French films. You were allowed to be something other than whatever it was that you did. But in the last few decades, a new idea has crept in: your job should be your passion, your purpose, your reason for being. It's not enough to be employed; you have to be inspired.

The culprit for all this? Advertising, of course. In the latter stages of the 20th century, advertising turned work into a lifestyle. If happiness could sell shampoo, some reasoned, then why not sell work too? A happy worker, the logic went, is a productive worker and, just as importantly, less likely to unionise.

So began a subtle but powerful rebranding campaign. The office was where you found your true calling. Jobs were sold on culture, mission and 'vibe', as well as salary. As Derek Thompson put it in *The Atlantic*, work in the 21st century has become 'a kind of religion, promising identity, transcendence and community'. Mission statements became sacred texts. Work and life merged.

In the process, work became far more invasive. You no longer left your job at the office. Your job followed you home, phoned you at dinner, emailed you overnight and haunted your dreams. Colleagues became your 'work family'. Offices were filled with beanbags, ping-pong tables, gyms and cafeterias. Some even offered laundry services and doggy day care. The message was clear: if your workplace has everything you need, why would you ever leave?

The rise of social media advice has only made things worse. Work should 'align with your values', harness your potential, contribute to society and look good on LinkedIn. You can't just show up and do the work – you must *live* your work, *love* your work, *be* your work. And if you're not fulfilled, the message is clear: you're doing it wrong.

So what's a person to do if they don't love their job and it doesn't bring them joy and fulfilment? Well, I'll tell you, my friend. They feel shit. They ask 'Why am I doing this?', 'Why am I so bored?', 'Why haven't I found my true calling?' and 'Am I wasting my life?'

The idea that work should be more than just a way to make money has created a society in which burnout is inevitable. Because when we're conditioned to believe that our jobs should make us happy, any sign of dissatisfaction starts to feel like a crisis. It's like expecting your toaster to also be your therapist. Or a kitchen sink to make your heart sing with joy.

Relatively speaking, the workers of the West don't really have all that much to complain about. We have just been conditioned to believe that work shouldn't feel like work.

But the sad fact, of course, is: it does.

19

LOVE HURTS

Why life isn't a rom-com (and never was)

Historically, love was considered too fragile
and unpredictable to be the foundation
of something as serious as marriage.
Alain de Botton, *The Course of Love*, 2016

I'm often told that the institution of marriage is in crisis. And the person saying it is not just my wife. Once the bedrock of Western civilisation, the nuclear family is quietly fizzling. As Stephanie Coontz points out, all over the Western world, 'marriage is no longer the central organising principle of people's lives. It's becoming just one lifestyle choice among many'. Or, to quote the journalist Rhaina Cohen, 'We have long seen romantic love as the peak experience of life, but a growing number of people are building meaningful, joyful, independent lives outside of that paradigm.' In other words, what was once seen as a rite of passage – as a routine pitstop on the road of life – is now like the Big Banana. You might check it out, if you're somewhere nearby, but there's certainly no reason to take a big detour. After all, there's a Big Potato and a Big Prawn somewhere else in the state, and if all else fails you can see the Big Poo. We've always been spoiled for big choices in this country – and marriage doesn't need to be one of them.

In the US, only 50 per cent of adults were married in 2021, down from 72 per cent in 1960. In Australia, the marriage rate has fallen to 3.6 per 1000 people, the lowest figure since World War I (when most eligible bachelors were busy being shot). The UK Office for National Statistics tells an even starker story: in Blighty, marriage rates are now at their lowest since 1862, way back when records began. In road-trip terms, it's like half the cars have already taken the exit to Singlehood and the rest are slowing down, trying to decide if they really want to pay the toll.

Even de facto relationships appear to be on the wane. According to the US Census Bureau, 38 per cent of American adults aged 25 to 54 are now unpartnered, up from 29 per cent in 1990. That's tens of millions of people actively opting out of coupledom and embracing what's now called 'conscious singlehood'. That's singlehood as Plan A, not Plan B. These people aren't broken down on the roadside waiting for a partner to pick them up; they've decided to keep driving solo, windows down, stereo up, and no arguments over where to stop for lunch. A 2022 Pew Research Center study found that 44 per cent of single Americans say they're not looking to date or be in a relationship at all. White picket fences are out. Self-fulfilment is very much in. For many, friends, pets, hobbies or purpose-driven work now offer the emotional fulfilment once expected from a spouse.

And then, of course, there are the incels: a subculture of angry young men who blame feminism for the fact that no one shags them. A full-blown cultural car crash lurking in some toxic corners of the internet, they're the kind of people who never quite learned how to drive – and now rage at women because their lives are a smoking ruin.

Plenty of married couples, meanwhile, are hitting reverse. Divorce rates are soaring all over the West, most especially among older couples. In the US, the divorce rate for people over 50 has doubled since 1990; for those over 65, it's tripled. Sociologists refer to this trend as the 'grey divorce' phenomenon – retirees realising, with grim clarity, that they'd rather die alone and be eaten by the cats than spend two more decades listening their spouse's views on the correct temperature for a thermostat, or that crap story about how they almost met Paul McCartney.

In short, the romantic script is being rewritten – or tossed out entirely. For some Westerners, marriage remains a goal. But for plenty of others, it's nothing more than a relic.

Now, in many ways, the decline of marriage is something to be celebrated, because it reflects a rise in freedom. For centuries, marriage wasn't so much a union of hearts as a locked boot you couldn't escape from. Not permitted to earn their own income, for most women staying unmarried wasn't a viable lifestyle choice, just a fast lane to poverty and disgrace.

Though for quite a few women, poverty may have been preferable. It's worth remembering that the word 'husband' comes from *húsbóndi*, or 'master', an Old Norse word that can also apply to a farmer who husbands his sheep. And that's more or less how marriage worked for centuries. A man owned and worked a woman in much the same way as he owned and worked everything else in his fields. Like a good ewe, a wife was expected to be obedient, fertile and useful. In return, she got 'protection', which, in this context, mostly meant not starving to death.

Just as farmers bred livestock to improve the herd, marriages were careful business arrangements designed to consolidate a family's land, wealth and power. You didn't marry for passion, just as you wouldn't buy a prize ram for his sparkling conversation. It was an agricultural arrangement and women were the livestock. The question wasn't 'Do I love them?' but 'How big is the dowry?', 'What's their family's political clout?' and 'Will this union keep our land from being annexed?'

Marriage wasn't about chemistry or the thrill of romance. It wasn't about happiness, fulfilment or finding your soulmate. Love, if it came along at all, was something that happened after the wedding. Or not, as the case may be. As Coontz puts it, 'For most of Western history, love and marriage were considered mutually exclusive.'

Even royalty – the people you'd assume had the most freedom to pick and choose – were caught in the same logic. A prince didn't marry a princess because she had long golden tresses and a good sense of humour. He married because she came with 2000 acres in Burgundy, a castle on the Rhine and a convenient truce with the French. If she also happened to be pleasant company, well, that was a bonus.

Love was lovely, if it happened. But, mostly, people just made do. Newlyweds didn't have long, heartfelt discussions about their favourite films or their complex range of emotional needs. Just a silent, lifelong agreement to share the same house and eventually pop out a couple of heirs.

So, yes, maybe it's a good thing that fewer people are racing to the altar these days. But if our expectations of relationships were a touch too low in the past, it's worth wondering if they've now soared too high. These days, it often seems we don't just want a partner; we want a soulmate, a best friend, a therapist, a chef, a maid, a wage earner and a sexual gymnast. Plus, someone who doesn't snore too much and generally remembers to take out the bins. The Belgian-American psychotherapist Esther Perel said it best: 'We come to one person and we are basically asking them to give us what once an entire village used to provide.'

Do I exaggerate? Maybe. But only slightly. As Swiss curmudgeon Denis de Rougemont points out, we've been sold a fairytale for decades: the myth of effortless, transcendent love – of lovers who never have to split a bill, unclog a toilet or inspect each other's rear ends for haemorrhoids. Disney movies groomed generations with 'happily ever after', where Cinderella, Snow White and Belle all bagged handsome princes who never once left their towels on the floor. *Pretty Woman* gave us billionaires with hearts of gold, *Notting Hill* sexy movie stars who loiter in bookstores. *Twilight* taught teenagers that stalking is a sign of devotion, *Titanic* that if you love someone it's okay to drown them. Meanwhile, *Bridgerton* threw in aristocrats with six-packs, and *Fleabag* gave us that piping-hot priest.

And Hollywood had help. De Beers convinced the world that 'a diamond is forever', while florists, chocolatiers and card-makers hammered home the idea that passion could be purchased in bulk. Hallmark industrialised Valentine's Day. Perfume ads promised that one sultry spritz would turn your pasty, balding bank-teller boyfriend into Antonio Banderas. Reality TV delivered love on tap, condensing 'lifelong commitment' into six weeks of poolside cocktail parties and hot-air-balloon dates. Throw in a few million pop songs – Whitney swearing she'll always love you, Bruno Mars offering to catch a grenade – and the message is clear: romance isn't rare or fragile, it's easy, common, and practically waiting for you at the checkout.

Then there's the wedding-industrial complex: a $70 billion global business. Your love apparently isn't real these days unless you're prepared to spend half a year's wage hiring out a winery, a drone photographer, a gelato cart and a three-tiered cake that costs more than a car. The illusion is that these props guarantee a perfect relationship – that if you buy the right package, the romance will take care of itself. Most couples begin married life with debt and a sense of mild disappointment. A sense that will only grow as the years drift by, filled with trips to IKEA and arguments about who should take out the bins.

In short, 'romance' is a bit of a pipedream – and this can be hard when we finally wake up. Because if and when a relationship doesn't tick every box, we start to wonder if we've made a mistake. We no longer judge relationships by a shared willingness to share food during winter but by a ruthless new metric. Does this person make me happy?

If the answer is anything less than an enthusiastic 'YES, YES, ONE THOUSAND TIMES YES!', the doubt and disdain can set in: Am I settling? Is this real love? Shouldn't it be more passionate, more fun, more … something? Maybe we're not really made for each other. Maybe we're not 'meant to be'. Maybe there's someone else who will make my soul sing.

A 2014 study in the *Journal of Family Psychology* found that people who held strong 'destiny beliefs' – that is, the idea that romantic partners are either 'meant to be' or not – were much more likely to report dissatisfaction in their relationships, particularly during times of conflict or stress. Such people were also more likely to give up on their relationships early, having interpreted normal friction as evidence of fundamental incompatibility. In other words, the more you believe in fairytale love, the more likely you are to be disappointed by reality.

Alain de Botton writes about this eloquently: 'We have been taught to expect love to be an ongoing source of joy and satisfaction. And when it inevitably fails to meet these unrealistic standards, we assume we've chosen the wrong partner.'

Adding to this problem, of course, are the dating apps. With an endless buffet of tasty options just one swipe away, it's all too easy to believe that something better is out there. As American psychologist Barry Schwartz explains in his 2004 book *The Paradox of Choice*, when people are faced with too many options, they become less satisfied with the one they've chosen, haunted by the spectre of alternatives. Apply that logic to dating and you get an entire generation swiping through potential soulmates like they're choosing a new pair of sneakers. Because there's always someone sexier, funnier, blonder, smarter, kinder, taller, richer and much better at stacking the dishwasher.

But here's the thing, folks. Even if that person actually exists, you can be pretty sure they'll suck at times too. The problem with real relationships is that they are forced to exist in real life. Even the healthiest, most functional marriages will occasionally involve pointless squabbles and watching your partner chew in a way that makes you wish they were dead. Some days, couples will argue about the correct way to vacuum. Other days, they will just sit in bored silence.

At the end of the day, the real problem isn't that marriage has changed. It's that our expectations of marriage have ballooned into something that no human being could ever possibly satisfy.

In any case, that's what I tell my wife!

20

FAMILY
BUSINESS

How we all got a bit weird about children

We've reached the point where a child's unhappiness
isn't just unfortunate – it's evidence that someone,
somewhere, didn't parent hard enough.
Jennifer Senior, *All Joy and No Fun*, 2014

If you ever want to feel better about your childhood, I suggest reading a Victorian-era memoir. Ideally, one that covers the author's time being systematically traumatised at a boarding school. Generally boasting names like Bleakminster College and all the warmth of a Siberian gulag, these were not places where young people were nurtured to blossom and thrive. They were places where beatings were routine, bullying was encouraged and the food may as well have been mucus.

Throw in cold showers, drafty halls, sex pests and neglect and you've got yourself an elite 19th-century British education. As one pupil at Rugby School recalled, 'The floggings were so frequent and so violent that the very memory of them made us tremble years later.' George Orwell, writing about his time at Eton, remembered being caned so hard that he bled through his trousers. School, he wrote, was a place of 'sneering, priggish, self-righteous' cruelty, where 'the business of boy-torture was carried out with the most gentlemanly and hypocritical manner imaginable'.

And kids' home lives weren't much better. If you were a member of the Victorian upper class, odds are you were raised by a nanny. The rule was that 'children are to be seen and not heard', but Victorian parents generally preferred they not be seen either. The aristocracy treated their offspring like pimples: unwelcome, painful and, all in all, best ignored. Even Queen Victoria herself described her childhood as 'melancholy' and 'miserable'. 'I was brought up very strictly,' she later recalled, 'and was not allowed to do anything that a child would enjoy.'

But lest you think the solution was to be one of the 'real people', let's not romanticise the life of the Victorian poor. Oliver Twist got off lightly. Sure, he was stuck in an orphanage with just the one bowl of gruel. But at least he wasn't stuck in a workhouse. Sort of like a prison, only less warm and cosy, these were places where kids could spend their time bricking coal or scrubbing latrines. If you were over 4 and had opposable thumbs, you were ready for work. Just ask the author Charles Dickens, who at age 12 was sent to work in a rat-infested factory after his father was jailed for debt. He later wrote, 'No words can express the secret agony of my soul as I sunk into this companionship of common men and boys.' Which is basically Victorian for 'my childhood was fucked'.

Do I have a point here? Yes, and once again it's all about the strangeness of modern expectations: specifically, the notion that childhood should be a magical time filled with innocence and wonder and joy. This vision isn't some eternal truth of human nature. It's a weird and relatively recent invention – right up there with reiki for dogs.

As English historian Hugh Cunningham writes, 'Childhood is not timeless. It is not universal. It is a changing idea, shaped by economic and social forces.' For most of history, no one particularly cared if children were happy. Childhood was less a golden era and more a short interlude between finishing up breastfeeding and finally working out how to be useful. You learned how to walk, you got strong enough to carry stuff and then you got handed a plough. Happiness was incidental, not essential.

Take ancient Rome. 'Roman children were largely invisible,' says Mary Beard, 'unless they were dying, inheriting or getting married.' Kids were only really considered if they were rich. And even then, 'childhood' ended roughly around the time your father decided you were ready to go to war or pop out a couple of kids.

In ancient Sparta, meanwhile, childhood was all about military onboarding. Newborn babies were inspected for physical defects and tossed off a cliff if they didn't pass muster. Boys were taken from their families at age 7 to live in barracks, where they were routinely beaten, starved and taught how to kill. Crying, needless to say, was discouraged. 'The boys are trained to bear pain and to conquer in battle,' Xenophon wrote. 'And in order to accustom them to this, they are whipped frequently, not for doing wrong, but to accustom them to bear pain.'

In medieval Europe, things weren't much better. French historian Philippe Ariès famously argued that 'in medieval society, the idea of childhood did not exist'. Essentially seen as second-rate farmers, children weren't precious seedlings in need of nurturing but flung headfirst into the worlds of work, war and wedlock as soon as their limbs could manage it. If you were old enough to walk, you were old enough to herd sheep, haul a bit of firewood or watch someone get hanged for stealing a goat. No one was tracking your 'developmental milestones', unless 'still alive at age 12' counted as a cause for celebration.

Childhood was like a waiting room for adulthood, preferably exited as quickly as possible. Nothing captures this better than medieval fairytales. Today, they're sweet stories full of twinkling forests, handsome princes, talking animals and glittering gowns.

But the original versions were less 'happily ever after' and more 'lasting psychological trauma'.

Take *Cinderella*. In the 1812 Brothers Grimm version, one stepsister cuts off her toes and the other her heel to squeeze into the glass slipper. Blood fills the shoe and birds peck out their eyes as punishment.

Or *Sleeping Beauty*. In Giambattista Basile's 17th-century tale *Sun, Moon and Talia*, the princess is raped in her sleep by a king and wakes only after giving birth to twins. There's no prince and no kiss. Just an open-and-shut case of assault.

Even *Little Red Riding Hood* ends in horror. In earlier versions, there's no woodcutter to save the day. The wolf eats Grandma, tricks Red into climbing into bed with him and promptly devours her too. The end.

And it wasn't just fairytales. Nursery rhymes were no picnic either. *Ring a Ring o' Roses* is widely believed to reference the plague: 'the roses' were the rash, 'a pocket full of posies' the herbal remedies to mask the stench of death and 'we all fall down' ... well, that one's fairly self-explanatory. Meanwhile, *Three Blind Mice* is actually about three Protestants who were conspiring against Bloody Queen Mary. In the end, they were caught, had their hands chopped off and were then burned alive at the stake.

Still not convinced? Look at the art. Medieval depictions of children are famously unsettling. They're not wide-eyed cherubs but shrunken, vaguely anxious adults. They don't giggle. They don't play. They just stand there like they're in the third hour of an all-day meeting and have just discovered they're behind in their taxes. Childhood, as we know it – innocent, sacred, protected, fun – was simply not a thing.

All that probably started to change in the 17th and 18th centuries, when a few Enlightenment thinkers took a look at children and started seeing something other than soldiers too weak to be sent off to war, or a wife slightly too young to shag. John Locke, for example, described children as a tabula rasa, a blank slate that could be shaped by experience and education.

Jean-Jacques Rousseau also helped lay the philosophical groundwork for the sentimental view of childhood that still lingers today. A man who abandoned all five of his children, and frequently paid prostitutes to give him a spank, he declared, 'Childhood has its own ways of seeing, thinking and feeling; nothing is less sensible than to try and substitute ours for theirs.' To Rousseau, children were morally superior: pure beings corrupted by the artificiality of adult society. 'Everything is good as it leaves the hands of the Author of things,' he wrote, 'everything degenerates in the hands of man.' It was, in many ways, the birth of the idealised childhood, as something protected, cultivated and cherished.

Still, it's worth noting that even the Enlightenment was more about theory than practice. Childhood may have been intellectually reimagined, but day to day it was still a rough gig.

Just ask Thomas Hardy's Little Father Time, who murders his siblings and hangs himself at age 7. Or the Little Match Girl, who freezes to death in the snow. In *Uncle Tom's Cabin*, Little Eva slowly wastes away from tuberculosis, while in *Little Women* it's scarlet fever that eventually does in young Beth. For his part, Dickens famously gave us the ever-coughing Little Nell, a fragile child-saint too pure for this world. (As Oscar Wilde famously said, 'One must have a heart of stone to read the death of Little Nell without laughing.')

In the 19th century, children's books were essentially cautionary tales, morality plays with a strong emphasis on fatal accidents, tragic orphans and nasty diseases.

But things did start to improve – at least for fictional children. By the Victorian era, the little ones on the page were no longer just coughing themselves to death in garrets; they were fast becoming cultural icons. Think sentimental portraits of cherubic orphans in lace bonnets. While real-life children were still being stuffed into chimneys or sent down coal mines, their rosy-cheeked fictional counterparts were hanging out with Peter Pan, Mr Toad, Winnie-the-Pooh and Margery Williams's Velveteen Rabbit. Soaked in innocence, imagination and syrupy sentiment, childhood in these books wasn't a preparation for life; it *was* life, in its purest, sweetest, stickiest form. There was no problem that a cuddle, a tea party or a toy couldn't fix. Even rabbits had rich inner lives.

Then came the 20th century. There were still plenty of belt-wielding fathers, don't get me wrong – and more than a few mothers whose main love was sherry – but something was shifting. Slowly, quietly, the gospel of happiness crept into the nursery.

A new idea began to take hold: maybe parenting was a serious job. Maybe children weren't just miniature adults waiting to be whipped into shape. Maybe – just maybe – they had unique needs.

Enter Sigmund Freud, with his theories about unconscious drives and early trauma. Enter Swiss psychologist Jean Piaget, with his neat stages of cognitive development. Childhood was no longer a biological waiting room for adulthood – it was a delicate psychological journey, filled with critical windows and sensitive phases, any one of which could be easily derailed. All of a sudden, children were fragile, complicated, in need of careful cultivation. Their innocence needed to be protected, their happiness ensured. Joy was their natural state, and anything less meant someone had screwed up.

And that someone, of course, was mum or dad. A sad child – once seen as the unfortunate byproduct of famine, plague or an unlocked bear cage – was now something far more ominous: a sign of bad parenting. If your child wasn't smiling, you were doing it wrong. Happiness became something children were expected to feel as a kind of emotional baseline. 'Happiness is as essential as food,' declared one early parenting manual. 'Make the child as happy as possible,' urged another, as if joy were a mechanical process involving levers and porridge.

In the 1930s, this cultural expectation had even found its anthem: 'Happy Birthday to You'. Sugary, simple and impossible to escape, the song became a compulsory fixture of family life. As American historian William Leach observed, 'Happiness was no longer a gift of fate – it was an entitlement to be engineered.'

By the 1940s, the 'happiness imperative' had sunk its teeth in so deep that even boredom got a makeover. Once seen as a natural byproduct of a long, slow afternoon, boredom was now a red flag. If your child was bored, it meant you hadn't stimulated them enough. You hadn't provided the right toys, experiences or enrichment. You had, in essence, failed to deliver joy on demand.

And as mass production and consumer capitalism took hold, the toy industry was more than happy to step in. Children became a target demographic with serious purchasing power – or at least serious pester power. The ideal postwar home morphed into a brightly lit command centre of delight, stocked with teddy bears, train sets, paint-by-numbers kits, miniature kitchens, junior carpentry sets and (ideally) one plastic pony per child.

By the 1960s, Australian kids had their own television shows (*Adventure Island, The Magic Circle Club, Skippy the Bush Kangaroo*), homegrown jingles and cereal mascots like Coco the Monkey and the Rice Bubbles trio: Snap, Crackle and Pop. The line between happiness and consumption blurred entirely. 'Make their eyes light up this Christmas,' promised one Myer Emporium catalogue. 'Nothing says joy like a new Matchbox car.' That was true for the kids, while for parents, of course, nothing said joy like a child quietly playing with said cars, so long as they were in another room far, far away.

By the 1980s, the stakes had risen again. Children now had Happy Meals, Saturday morning cartoons, sticker albums, Transformers with detachable missiles, Care Bears, Cabbage Patch Dolls and a growing mountain of anxiety around 'screen time'.

Which brings us to today. Childhood is now a project, complete with KPIs, benchmarks, sensory-play outcomes, enrichment strategies and regular emotional check-ins. And if your child isn't smiling through it all? That's on you.

Modern parents spend more time with their children than any generation in history, and yet they're constantly told it's not enough. Not baking enough organic muffins. Not providing enough 'support'. Not logging enough 'quality time', even after sitting through six fucking Wiggles songs, explaining how clouds work and building a Lego metropolis.

The pressure isn't just to be good – it's to be *great*. Warm but firm. Playful but structured. Emotionally available and educationally on-trend. A hybrid of therapist, chef, tutor and improv comedian.

Today, childhood comes with its own philosophies, its own hashtags, its own aesthetic. There are bedtime mindfulness apps. Junior yoga mats. Toddler probiotics. Montessori toys made of sustainably harvested pine. And entire aisles at Kmart devoted to its ever-shifting mood board.

Parents are responsible for delivering a steady stream of joy, calm, stimulation and age-appropriate development. The goal is no longer to raise a reasonably decent human being who doesn't become a serial killer; it's to produce a well-read, musically gifted, emotionally articulate, STEM-proficient, socially capable genius who eats all their veggies, plays heaps of sport and feels *happy every step of the way.*

The modern child must be creative but calm, social but independent, expressive but tidy. And 10,000 per cent sugar-free. To that end, a toddler's mood can now be tracked, diagnosed, managed and monetised. There are books, blogs, TED talks and entire parenting frameworks with names like *Conscious Discipline, The Gentle Parenting Book, Raising Good Humans* and *Respectful Parenting.* What used to be a mix of instinct, folk wisdom and 'just do what your mum did' has become a commercially saturated pressure cooker.

Of course, all this focus on childhood happiness hasn't made parents happier. In fact, quite the opposite. As Jennifer Senior once quipped, 'We expend so much energy trying to make our kids happy that we often forget to enjoy them.'

According to a 2023 Pew Research study, 62 per cent of parents say parenting is 'harder than they expected', and one in four mothers report being *very* stressed. Fathers aren't far behind, with 18 per cent saying the same. Meanwhile, Gallup has found that parents of young children in high-income countries routinely report lower life satisfaction than their child-free peers, suggesting that the 'parenting equals fulfilment' formula might be oversold.

And it's competitive. Fuck me dead, it's competitive. From the smug mum in your parenting WhatsApp group to the other smug mum in your parenting WhatsApp group, there's always someone doing it better. There's always someone putting sushi in their lunchbox, plus a serving of kale, and teaching them how to play violin in about six different languages. A 2018 survey by the American CS Mott Children's Hospital found that 43 per cent of parents felt judged by other parents 'all or most of the time'.

So here we are. After centuries of largely ignoring children's happiness, we've overcorrected to the point where it now feels compulsory. Childhood joy has become a full-blown production, and, like any ambitious production, someone has to foot the bill. That someone, more often than not, is the parent: exhausted, guilty, anxious and quietly wondering whether all this curated happiness is actually making *anyone* feel happy at all.

21

ALL BY MYSELF

How social media turned joy into a blood sport

Comparison is the thief of joy.

Unknown

For the vast majority of human existence, we have lived our lives in tiny little tribes. Groups of sixty or so people, maybe half of them relatives, our constant companions around campfires and caves. And for about 10,000 years after that, we tended to live in tiny little villages. Population: a few hundred souls. You knew the butcher, the baker and the candlestick maker. Plus the leper, the prostitute, the local sex pest and that hideous crone with the warts. You might meet a few strangers at the annual market or when a wandering minstrel passed through town with some brand-new disease. But, all things considered, that was about it. From birth to death, from the cradle to the grave, your entire social network – your entire exposure to the outside world – consisted of about 300 people. Tops.

And even as recently as the early 20th century, things weren't too different. Most people could go their whole life in daily contact with just a few people. And they could generally avoid most of them by taking the long way to the shops.

Nowadays, however, introverts aren't quite so lucky. We've got planes, trains and automobiles; emails and texts; FaceTime, Tinder, Slack, X and LinkedIn. Not to mention roughly 1400 WhatsApp groups that we never asked to be part of, but which we still hear from 245 times a day. All while we scroll through 'friend suggestions' on

Facebook and receive birthday wishes from some rando guy who apparently went to our school. The average human has never been more connected. We are absolutely swimming in people.

And yet the average person also appears to be drowning. In anxiety, stress and despair. Could it be that having all these seemingly happy people in our lives is part of the problem? That the tyranny of expectation is once again being felt?

Maybe. Hear me out. Once upon a time, you only had to compare yourself to those few hundred people in your village, most of whom had scurvy and less than three teeth. Sure, social comparisons existed. People would put on their best tunics or jerkins for feast days and probably make an effort to hide their worst pustule. But, for your average peasant, looking fabulous just wouldn't have been on the agenda. Life was a relentless cycle of tilling, harvesting, sneezing and coughing, and no one expected you to do it with style. If your rags were intact and more or less free of lice, you were pretty much ahead of the game.

Even as recently as the 1980s, you generally had to attend a school reunion to feel completely inadequate – or maybe visit a distant relative who had 'made it big'. Your chances of seeing a stranger's six-pack were minimal and you rarely caught a glimpse of their stylish décor.

Now, however, we see six-packs every day. Thanks to social media, feelings of inadequacy are now available on demand, for free and delivered straight to our phones. We're no longer just comparing ourselves to the people in our neighbourhood – we're comparing ourselves to the entire planet. You can be sipping coffee in reasonably clean boxer shorts, only to scroll past a 22-year-old millionaire doing yoga on a yacht. You can be wondering if you've paid the rent, then discover that Becky from high school has just bought her third house. Before you've even gone to the toilet, you've seen sunrise workouts, artfully plated brunches, engagement rings, exciting promotions, relationship milestones, happy families and parties that you weren't invited to – all sent your way with a series of #blessed captions by people 'living the dream'.

Social media has turned well-being into a competitive sport, and not too many people want to look like they're losing. So we adapt. We perform happiness. We smile wide and post selectively. The internet doesn't want your melancholy – no one's rushing to 'like' a post about 2am existential dread or a weekend spent in the same tracksuit eating toast.

Because visibility is the game, people post their wins: the tropical holiday, the promotion, the engagement ring with a sunset background. A post about feeling vaguely rubbish? Not exactly algorithm-friendly. Nobody's double-tapping 'Still bloated from Tuesday's lasagne' or 'Day three of mysterious rash'.

So we edit, filter and polish our lives into highlight reels. We create a world in which everyone is thriving. Even if, behind the scenes, they're quietly Googling how to fake their own death.

The problem isn't that these moments are fake – they're just *selective*, carefully edited highlights presented as the whole story. But the more we see them, the more we mistake the highlight reel for reality. We start to believe that life should always be effortless, exciting and emotionally fulfilling. And when our own lives don't match up, we feel defective.

When everyone online looks like they're crushing life, your very normal, very reasonable Wednesday can suddenly feel like a failure.

You catch yourself wondering: *Should I be doing more? Going out more? Having more fun? Making more friends? When did I start doing life wrong? And where the hell can I buy a yacht?*

And the research backs this up. A 2012 study of US students by Hui-Tzu Chou and Nicholas Edge found that the more time people spend on social media, the more likely they are to believe others have better lives. Participants who spent more time on Facebook were significantly more likely to agree with statements like 'Others are happier than me' and 'Life is unfair'. The more they scrolled, the more they internalised the illusion that everyone else was richer, busier, thinner, more popular and more fulfilled – and that they had somehow fallen short.

Even when our lives are objectively good, constant comparison makes us feel like we've missed a crucial memo on how to be happy. One moment you're tapping through someone's brunch pics, the next you're questioning your job, your haircut, your great anecdote about the pumpkin and whether or not you peaked in Year 10. This is the modern paradox: we are more connected than ever – and more convinced that we're falling behind.

And this is not just a theory. In 2019, Jean Twenge, Gabrielle Martin and W R Campbell laid it out bluntly in their study *Increases in Depression, Self-Harm and Suicide Among US Adolescents After 2010*. The more time people spend glued to screens, the worse they tend to feel. Analysing data from over 200,000 US teens, they found that rates of depressive symptoms, self-harm and suicide spiked dramatically after 2010, just as smartphones and social media went mainstream. 'Adolescents who spent more time on electronic devices were significantly more likely to report mental health issues,' they wrote, 'while those who spent more time on non-screen activities – such as in-person social interaction, sports and exercise – were less likely.'

It's also worth noting that, despite the planet being jam-packed with eight billion people, loneliness has never been more common. Surveys across the US, the UK and Europe suggest more than half of adults feel rather lonely. The World Health Organization calls it a public health crisis.

But maybe loneliness today isn't about feeling alone so much as about feeling out of step. Scroll through Instagram, TikTok or Snapchat and you're bombarded with curated highlight reels that make it look as if everyone else is in an episode of *Friends*. Against that backdrop, an ordinary Friday night watching Netflix with your dog and a packet of chips can feel like a sad, lonely failure.

For some, it's no longer enough just to have friends – you're supposed to see them often, connect deeply, laugh effortlessly and then post the receipts. Friendship has shifted from something you feel to something you perform, a kind of social proof that you're winning at life. When our actual, slightly messy, perfectly decent friendships don't stack up against the digital theatre, it's easy to presume we're missing out. As science writer Lydia Denworth notes, we've romanticised friendship to the point of absurdity: 'We have come to expect friendships to be ideal and constant and filled with shared secrets and socialising.'

Real friendships don't usually look like that. Sometimes they're quiet. Sometimes they lag. Sometimes they're just two bored people trying to play Scrabble and wondering if it would be rude to go home. Sometimes weeks or months go by without catching up, because people are tired, broke or have a bad back. Sometimes it's years because ... well ... time flies.

But you don't see *that* version of friendship on Instagram. Instead, you see the curated montage: the festivals, the dinner parties, the handwritten birthday cards; the hilarious leotard Elle wore to Jazzercise. And then you look at your own life – at the chips, at the couch, at what could well be a pee stain – and you start to wonder, *What am I doing wrong?*

The answer is *nothing*. I promise. You're fine. Other people aren't happy and popular 24/7. They are just better at posting.

22

BOULEVARD OF BROKEN DREAMS

Why sadness is an important part of life's journey

Tears are words that need to be written.

Paulo Coelho, *Aleph*, 2010

The world is full of useless books. I'm not just talking about celebrity memoirs or some crappy novel about teenage vampires. I'm talking about the 'serious' stuff too. Weighty tomes like Jean Baudrillard's *Simulacra and Simulation* or Hegel's *The Phenomenology of Spirit*. The sorts of books that ask you whether reality is real and then spend 600 pages making sure you don't care. Books written just to give academics their tenure and to bore all the students they teach.

You could be forgiven for thinking that this book is equally useless. Another exercise in complicated nitpicking. Another collection of thousands of words that somehow manage to say nothing at all.

After all, if pursuing happiness is such a bad idea, what is the alternative? Are we meant to pursue unhappiness, like holidaying in the Gold Coast, binge-watching *The Masked Singer* or swapping champagne for arsenic? Am I saying we should all dim the lights, stab ourselves in the thigh and weep slow, silent tears of despair?

Of course not. I'm not saying that anyone should actively chase sadness. I'm just saying it's going to catch up with all of us from time to time, whether we like it or not. As the poet Waldo Emerson oh-so-poetically wrote, 'I pack my trunk, embrace my friends, embark on the sea and at last wake up in Naples and there beside me is the stern fact, the sad self, unrelenting, identical, that I fled from.' You can book a ticket to paradise, but your brain will still come along for the ride.

Occasional sadness is simply a price we pay for being alive, sentient and conscious. It's all part of the human package. Every life, even a charmed one, is stuffed to the gills with despair. With pain. With loss. With disappointment. With sickness. With the peculiar agony of having to update your wi-fi password or listen to elevator music when you're 'on hold'. As Shakespeare once wrote (because that guy knew his stuff), 'The web of our life is of a mingled yarn, good and ill together.' In other words, life isn't a seamless tapestry of joy; it's a patchwork quilt – part silk, part hessian sack, with lice and one or two moth holes. So when sadness knocks, it's coming in anyway. As psychologist Susan David says, 'Discomfort is the price of admission to a meaningful life.'

Now, that doesn't mean you should roll out a welcome mat and let sadness move in. Like any guest, it's fine for a visit but a nightmare as a flatmate. Left unchecked, it curdles into self-pity. Every missed train, every unanswered text becomes further proof of a grand cosmic conspiracy against you. Like an anti-vaxxer during a COVID lockdown, you eventually become the misunderstood hero in a one-person tragedy – a play in which life is cruel, the universe unjust and only *you* see the world as it is.

Take Miss Havisham, the famously heartbroken figure from Charles Dickens's *Great Expectations*, who essentially invited sadness to live in her head. After being jilted at the altar, she retreats into her crumbling mansion for decades. She stops all the clocks, leaves her wedding feast to rot on the table and never, ever takes off the dress.

Her grief doesn't give her insight – it gives her inertia. She is curating her heartbreak like a museum exhibit.

Or if you want a metaphor with a bit more brimstone, why not check out Dante's *Inferno*? As the reader descends through the various circles of hell – the upper ones reserved for adulterers and liars, the lower ones for traitors and murderers – they eventually reach the very centre. And there sits Satan.

'The emperor of the sorrowful realm' isn't an impressive figure. Far from being a fiery overlord commanding legions, the prince of darkness is trapped and frozen. He doesn't roar or rage. He wallows and sulks. Utterly consumed by various slights and regrets, Satan is far and away the saddest figure in Dante's famous 14th-century poem, a monument to self-absorption so complete it literally traps him in hell.

So yes, sadness can deepen you. But only if you let it pass through you. Holding onto it too tightly keeps you stuck. You're not grieving anymore; you're decorating your own prison.

The opposite mistake is pretending no one's knocking. When misery comes to the door, some people turn off the lights and hide behind the couch. But ignored guests don't vanish; they become squatters. As the Dutch psychiatrist Bessel van der Kolk warns, 'Ignoring our emotions is a great way to guarantee that they will later come out in uglier, more distorted forms.'

Back in the 1980s, Harvard psychologist Daniel Wegner demonstrated this with his now-famous white bear experiment. Participants were told *not* to think about a white bear for five minutes. The result, of course, was that they couldn't stop. The more they tried to suppress the thought, the more their minds fixated on it.

Wegner's conclusion? When we attempt to suppress a thought, part of our brain constantly checks to see if we're succeeding, which, paradoxically, brings the thought back into focus. The harder you push down a thought, the more it will pop back up.

And emotions work the same way. Suppress sadness and it ferments, bubbling back in weird, toddler-like tantrums until you're forced to drink heavily (or, I guess, try to deal with it).

So maybe – just maybe – the trick isn't to push sadness away or make it too comfortable. It's to respect it. Let it sit with you for a bit. Treat it like that chatty neighbour you can't escape – the one who loves to regale you with accounts of their cat's UTI. You don't love it, but you nod politely, endure the monologue and eventually they shuffle off, satisfied they've shared their truth.

And this, increasingly, is what psychologists are shouting from rooftops: our cultural obsession with pathologising every emotional dip is making things worse. We treat every pang of sadness like it requires a prescription, every wobble like it's breaking news. We slap labels, apps and mindfulness subscriptions on feelings that might just need a cup of tea and a sulk. In our frantic rush to *fix* sadness, we've forgotten how to just *feel* it – and let it do its small, grubby job.

In their 2002 classic *Very Happy People*, psychologists Ed Diener and Martin Seligman found something that should have been blindingly obvious: even the happiest people have crap days. They still miss trains. They still get gastro. They still wonder where it all went wrong. The only thing that makes them 'different' is that they don't take such days to heart. They don't see sadness as a *malfunction*. They don't spiral at the first sign of discomfort. Sadness, for such people, isn't a crisis; it's just another part of life's deal.

The Stoics got this centuries ago. Marcus Aurelius – Roman emperor, reluctant philosopher and patron saint of existential sighing – put it best: 'The wise man accepts his pain, endures it, but does not add to it.' In other words, feel your pain but don't feed it. Don't panic. Don't wallow. Don't drown it in shame. Don't smother it with self-help and tai chi. Just nod politely, offer it a chair and wait for it to leave. Chances are, it very soon will.

In 2012, psychologist Iris Mauss and her colleagues set out to test a curiously modern paradox: what happens when people really, *really* want to be happy? Interestingly, she found that the more people valued happiness and treated it like a personal project, a measure of success or an emotional KPI, the less happy they actually felt. She said, 'The more people want to be happy, the more likely they'll be disappointed.' Or, as she later wrote, 'Valuing happiness may lead people to be less happy just when happiness is within reach.'

In other words, turning happiness into a goal tends to backfire, like trying to fall asleep by reminding yourself just how badly you need to fall asleep. Or, worse, trying to shit on cue. Just like your bowels, happiness works best when left to do its thing without constant monitoring.

Because when you *expect* to be happy, you start tracking your mood like it's a stock price. Instead of simply enjoying a moment, you start evaluating it. You second-guess yourself. Am I happy enough? Should I be happier than this? Why don't I feel like that complete prat on Instagram who keeps on announcing she's #blessed?

It's the emotional equivalent of chasing a butterfly. The harder you run, the further it floats. The tighter you grip the idea of happiness, the more sharply you feel its absence. And that's the real tragedy. When you treat sadness as a personal failure, you double the burden. You're not just sad – you're ashamed of being sad. You feel like you've failed some kind of invisible exam. So next time sadness shows up, don't panic. Don't tell it to leave. Let it in. Let it talk. Let it be.

23

YOU CAN'T ALWAYS GET WHAT YOU WANT

But that's okay

Sorrow is one of the vibrations that prove the fact of living.
Antoine de Saint-Exupéry, French writer

Do you remember that misery-as-a-chatty-neighbour metaphor from a few pages back? It was rather a good one, even if I do say so myself. But strap yourself in, my friend, for the time has come to give you an even better one. Ready? Okay. Here goes. A bit of sadness, now and then, is like a spell of crappy weather. It's cold, wet and windy, and it soaks everything in sight, but eventually it moves on.

Obviously, nobody *likes* rain. It ruins your hair, messes with picnics, slows down traffic and dampens your mood. It's inconvenient, unpredictable and faintly depressing. But when it rains, do we scream at the sky? Try to hurl the water back into the clouds? Send an angry email to the Bureau of Meteorology? Do we buy a book about 'manifesting dryness'? Blame our parents? Decide that, in some way, it's all our fault, some sort of reflection on our worth as a person? No, of course not. We just wait the rain out. Or throw on a parka and get on with our day.

Emotional weather works the same way. There's not much use trying to predict it. There's no use trying to stop it. And it makes no sense to take it personally. Sad times are always going to come along, whether you like it or not, just as storms are always going to roll through. Neither of these things mean that you're broken. They just mean that you're living on Earth.

But here's the thing that makes this metaphor so damn good. (Congratulations, Eamon, you've gone and done it again.) As inconvenient as it is, human beings *need* rain. Without rain, nothing would grow. There'd be no blossoms, no colour, no trees, no fruit. The world would be dust, sand and rocks.

I'm sure you know what's coming next. It's that emotional rain bears fruit too. Those grey days help you grow. Misery waters parts of us we can't yet see: the deep parts, the stubborn roots, the green shoots of wisdom and humour. It washes dirty old things away and sets the stage for something new to break through.

Sad things are like those horrible gym exercises that hurt like fuck but, over time, somehow make you feel better.

And if you realise this, you'll probably feel better still. In a 2016 study in *Emotion*, researchers gave smartphones to 365 Germans aged 14 to 88 and pinged them six times a day for three weeks. Each ping was a mini emotional check-in. Were they happy? Sad? Anxious? Irritated? Quietly seething because they didn't get enough sleep? They were also asked about whether their mood swings felt meaningful or just mildly annoying. And here's what the researchers found: people who believed negative emotions had *value* – that sadness, anger or anxiety might actually serve a purpose – were less affected by them. Their bad moods didn't hit as hard. Their mental health didn't take a dive.

So if you think sadness is a useful thread in the fabric of life, then it probably will be. If you think it's a hole or a tear, then there's every chance you'll be correct. As one of the study's authors, psychologist Dr Maya Tamir, put it, 'People want to feel very good all the time in Western cultures – but that may not be very realistic or healthy.'

So to specifics: what benefits, you ask, can misery give us? Plenty, I reply, twirling my cane with a debonair flourish guaranteed to win the admiration of all passers-by. Here are just a few of the juicy fruits that feeling sad helps to grow.

Misery Makes You Human

Imagine, for a moment, that you're about to have a baby. First of all, let me just say congratulations! Now, if you're anything like most parents-to-be, I'm sure you don't really care if your kid grows up to be an artist, an accountant, a builder or a rollerblader. (Okay, fine, maybe you don't want them to be an accountant. But I feel like my general point stands.) You just want them to be happy, right? Because that's all that really matters at the end of the day.

If that's the case, good for you! That's absolutely lovely. Rather warms me old heart.

Or rather, it *would* be lovely if it wasn't a total lie. 'A lie?' you say. 'A lie!' I repeat. Because what if I told you that non-stop, permanent happiness for your child could be achieved with one simple trick. We take your newborn baby ('Eamon' is a nice name) and put them on a heroin drip. From birth to death, little Eamon could be kept in a state of uninterrupted, chemically induced, vitamin-rich bliss. A state of brainless, wordless, wriggly euphoria. Best of all, they'd live a life with no problems. A life with no tears, no tantrums, no bullies, no broccoli, no sunburn or broken bones. They'd have no pimples and no puberty. No homework and no heartbreak. They would never have to do a detention. They'd never get caught having a wank.

Technically speaking, that's a very happy life. But it's also the stuff of a horror film. No one, *absolutely no one*, would want that for their child. And you'd have to be pretty clinically depressed to ever want such a life for yourself.

The problem with constant 'happiness' is the premise of Aldous Huxley's 1932 novel *Brave New World*. He imagined a society so obsessed with stability that it had found a way to eradicate suffering. The citizens of the World State live in a drugged, dulled state of contentment thanks to a government-issued pill. Their lives have everything – comfort, convenience, order – except joy or meaning. Because meaning comes from struggle. From contrast. From the parts of life that *hurt*.

And just in case you think my cultural references are a touch out of date, let me point out that this problem is part of *The Matrix*. As Agent Smith patiently explains to Keanu (who, as ever, looks like he's just been concussed), the Matrix simulation was originally designed to be a perfect world where everyone was happy. But it flopped spectacularly. The problem wasn't the coding, it was the people. We humans could tell that something was off and, as a result, kept on trying to wake up. 'Human beings define their reality through suffering and misery,' Smith sighs. The moment that everything goes right is the very moment things begin to feel wrong.

Which brings us to an awkward truth: happiness *isn't* actually what we're all after. Maybe what we really want, deep down, whether we admit it or not, is the *full spectrum* of human experience. The whole enchilada. The full guacamole of joy and grief, triumph and heartbreak. A big heaping plate of life's fajitas, however hot and spicy they may sometimes be.

To *feel* fully alive, we have to *feel things*, full stop. Sadness is what provides the flavour of our days. It pushes us to reflect, to connect, to care. And in a strange, roundabout way, it often guides us straight towards the things that make life worth living.

John Stuart Mill said it best: 'It is better to be a human being dissatisfied than a pig satisfied.' Translation? It's better to live a complicated, sometimes painful existence than to drift through life in a blissful fog. Because you can't selectively numb pain without numbing joy. Emotions don't come with a 'just the fun bits' filter. Suppress the sadness and you suppress the love, the desire, the laughter, the awe. The moments that *matter* – falling in love, finishing something difficult, reconnecting with a family member or friend – only feel good because of what came before: the fear, the doubt, the ache.

We want joy, but only because we've known sorrow. We crave success, but only because we've tasted failure. We treasure love, but only because we know what it feels like to lose it – or fear that we might. A life without sadness, without longing, without uncertainty, would not be a life. Misery is not proof that something's wrong. It is proof that you are alive.

Misery Makes You Interesting

Have you ever noticed that (present company excluded, of course) incredibly good-looking people can sometimes be a touch boring? Not always, but more often than not the unbearably attractive are merely that: attractive. And that's where their CV ends. Take someone like Megan Fox. She. Is. Hot. Hubba hubba. Ay caramba. Va va voom.

Lord have mercy. Et cetera, et cetera, et cetera. But just try making it through one of Megan's interviews without slipping into a coma. Gwyneth Paltrow, by the same token, is about as exciting as toast, while Tom Cruise is like a lecture on tax law.

There's a reason for this. When your breasts, biceps or bone structure do a heap of heavy lifting, life doesn't always demand a great personality. Strangers will still smile. Colleagues will still be charmed. Friends will still laugh at your jokes. You don't need all that much in the way of wit, verve or depth, so there's a sporting chance you'll end up without them.

Meanwhile, the rest of us have been hard at work. We've been sharpening our banter, polishing our jokes and workshopping anecdotes that hopefully say 'charming' rather than 'sad cry for help'. In short, we've had to *try*.

But this logical connection doesn't just stop at looks. It applies to anyone who drifts through life unbruised. People who've never suffered rarely have much to say.

Happiness without hardship is like soup without salt. Technically fine, but bland, forgettable and lacking bite. Nobody wants a dinner party anecdote about someone who's happily married, thriving at work and still finds time for Pilates. Where's the grit?

Misery, by contrast, has texture. It gives you perspective. And stories. And scars. George Eliot once called pain 'a new mysterious inlet of self-knowledge'. That's why your most emotionally literate friends aren't the ones whose lives look like an ad. They're the ones who've cried in stairwells. Who've been cracked open by life and stitched themselves back together. Slowly. Clumsily. Honestly.

Because pain may sting, but it also gives you material, something to say besides, 'We're thinking of doing a reno.'

And if you've somehow ended up both beautiful and interesting? Well, then. Congratulations. Everyone secretly hates you.

Misery Builds Character

There's an old truism – beloved by business columnists – that goes something like this: 'The first generation builds it. The second maintains it. The third blows it all on cocaine.' Or, as the Americans say, 'From shirtsleeves to shirtsleeves in three generations.'

The message? Hardship builds muscle and comfort turns it to flab. Things only grow stronger when stressed. You don't build resilience when life is served on a silver platter. You build it through emotional push-ups, psychological burpees and the kind of life squats that make you cry in the shower. Because life will hit you: it'll delay your flights, delete your Word docs, misplace your phone charger and ruin your sandwich. But every time you get back up – bloodied, winded, heartbroken, whatever – you will, in some way, have grown.

We *say* we value grit. We put it in books and on mugs. But as a culture, we're increasingly allergic to the one thing that builds it: suffering. The Stoics, of course, understood this. Just as you lift weights to build muscle, you lift misfortune to build wisdom. They even had a phrase: *amor fati* – love your fate. Not endure it. Love it. Lost your job? Congrats, you've been promoted to Advanced Resilience. Got dumped? That's an emotional deadlift. Tried to impress someone with your dance moves and face-planted? Plyometric humility. Farted during a eulogy? A masterclass in core vulnerability. Accidentally sent a nude to your nan? Radical acceptance: complete. As Seneca said, 'Difficulties strengthen the mind, as labour does the body.'

Nietzsche was more poetic: 'You must be ready to burn yourself in your own flame. How could you rise anew if you have not first become ashes?'

And this isn't just philosophers; it's scientists, too. In the 1990s, psychologists Richard Tedeschi and Lawrence Calhoun coined 'Post-Traumatic Growth' after finding that survivors of major crises often reported sharper appreciation for life, stronger relationships and deeper resilience. Later studies confirmed it: moderate misfortune – the kettlebell kind, not the spine-crushing kind – acts like emotional weight training. Too little stress and you stay fragile. Too much and you snap. But a few bruises along the way? That's character-building.

History is full of shredded spirits forged through hardship:

- Nelson Mandela spent twenty-seven years in prison and came out curling barbells of forgiveness. 'I never lose,' he said. 'I either win or learn.'
- Abraham Lincoln buried two sons, lost his mother at nine, wrestled depression and still stitched together a nation at war with itself. Sadness wasn't weakness – it was his core strength.
- Winston Churchill battled Nazis abroad and depression at home: 'If you're going through hell, keep going.'
- JK Rowling was a broke single mum scribbling in cafes. Out of despair came a billion-dollar empire (which she now uses to bully trans people). 'Rock bottom,' she said, 'became the

solid foundation on which I rebuilt my life.' That's not a rock bottom; that's a squat rack.

- Oprah Winfrey overcame childhood abuse and poverty to become a global powerhouse. 'Where there is no struggle, there is no strength.' She's bench-pressing millions.
- Stephen Colbert lost his father and two brothers in a plane crash at 10. Out of tragedy came comedy with muscle – deadlifts of despair turned into punchlines.
- Michael Jordan was cut from his high-school team. He didn't fold. He trained. 'I've failed over and over and over again. That is why I succeed.' No air balls, no Air Jordan.
- Steve Jobs was fired from Apple, hit rock bottom, then came back with the iPhone. Most of us get sacked and sit around in pyjamas. Jobs turned redundancy into CrossFit for the soul.

The pattern's clear: no gains without pain. No grit without failure. No emotional abs without heartbreak squats. If you're hurting, you're evolving.

Welcome to the Gym of Life. Membership is compulsory, the equipment is weird and the trainers are mostly tragic figures from history. Some days you're bench-pressing heartbreak. Other days you're stuck on the treadmill of minor inconveniences. But every set, every rep, every tear builds strength you won't notice until the weight gets heavier. That's the hidden upside of suffering: the bruises are proof you're building muscle.

And one day, without even realising it, you'll look back at the weight you've lifted – grief, failure, rejection – and notice something weird. You're not just surviving. You're strong.

Misery Can Make You Appreciative

Even though he didn't actually exist, Sisyphus feels strangely real. In the myths, he was an ancient Greek king who lied to the gods, which is not a move I would recommend. In return, he was handed a punishment that's basically the blueprint for hellish pointlessness: to spend eternity and beyond rolling a boulder up a hill, only to have it tumble back down at the end of each day. No progress, no variety, no chance of a smaller rock. Just endless heaving, sweating, slipping and swearing. To make matters worse, he knew that the rock would always win. That he was stuck in an infinite loop of futility, like someone trying to get planning permission from Yarra Council.

Having worked in the public service, I have to say that I know just how he feels. Most of life is repetitive, thankless and faintly ridiculous. We wake up. We load the dishwasher. We work. We send emails. We unload the dishwasher. We answer more emails. Just when we think we've reached the top, the boulder slips and we're back at the bottom, trying to remember our wi-fi password.

French existentialist Albert Camus loved the myth of Sisyphus – and agreed that in effect it was no myth at all. In a famous 1942 essay, he argued that we should all embrace the ultimate futility of our actions, because 'the struggle itself toward the heights [should be] enough to fill a man's heart. One must imagine Sisyphus happy.'

Happiness comes from learning to roll with the boulder during its ups and its downs, to find meaning in the pain and the climb. A 2013 study in *The Journal of Positive Psychology* found that people who'd experienced moderate adversity – not tragedy, just a few metaphorical faceplants –reported greater life satisfaction than those who'd breezed through unbruised. Japanese-American psychologist Shigehiro Oishi dubbed it the 'adversity sweet spot'. In other words, the Goldilocks Zone of Suffering: not too much, not too little. Just enough to make socks fresh from the dryer feel like a miracle.

Turns out the most content people aren't the ones with glowing skin – they're the ones who've been knocked flat just enough times to stop taking the sunshine for granted. Because once you've pushed your own boulder, joy stops being wallpaper. You taste your coffee. You smell the roses. You forgive your cousin for that thing he said in 2014.

It's why people who've been broke tend to appreciate money more than trust fund kids. It's why refugees often cherish things like working heaters more than a billionaire does his third yacht. It's why second marriages are statistically more stable than first ones.

Even aging follows this logic. The famous U-curve of happiness, confirmed in studies across more than seventy countries, shows that people get happier as they get older. Expectations finally loosen their death grip. You stop caring so much about the top of the hill. You start to enjoy the shove.

That's the quiet magic of misery. It's not very glamorous. It kind of hurts your back. But in a world constantly shouting for more money, more hustle, more biceps, more *more*, misery has the audacity to whisper, 'Maybe, just the climb is enough.'

Misery Can Make You Kinder

Imagine being someone who's never been sick or poor. Someone who's never lost a pet, got a nosebleed while flirting or been forced to watch a friend perform in a play. Sounds amazing, right? Wrong. What you're imagining here is a sociopath, and not the sexy, brooding, mysterious kind. More like the *call-the-police-and-hide* kind.

Misery is how the heart stretches. It's how we grow empathy, humility and the ability to laugh at ourselves. It's how we build character, stay kind and keep human. Without sadness, without friction, without rejection or doubt, the average human being would basically turn into Piers Morgan. All ego. No empathy. Unbearable.

History, alas, is full of such people.

Take Caligula, one of the first Roman emperors. Raised in obscene privilege and regarded as a god, he grew up swaddled in silk, jewels and worship. With nothing resembling a reality check, he spiralled into grotesque cruelty. Suetonius describes him 'delighting in torture' and 'inventing new kinds of cruelty'. He had senators forced to run for miles beside his chariot until they collapsed. He once ordered an entire section of a stadium crowd thrown to the wild beasts simply because he was bored. He executed men for telling jokes, or looking at him the wrong way, and sometimes forced parents to watch their children's executions, then dine at his table. That's what happens when pampering meets power.

Not long after came Nero, another imperial nepo baby. Handed an empire at 16, Caligula was called 'a monster with the features of a man' by Tacitus, and history seems to suggest he had a point. Among other career highlights, Nero executed his stepbrother, had his own mother stabbed to death and kicked his pregnant wife Poppaea to death during an argument. He's even said to have had Christians dipped in pitch and set on fire, because he felt that some living torches might really light up his garden.

Fast-forward a couple of millennia and we have Uday Hussein, Saddam's eldest son. Pampered with fleets of Ferraris, private zoos and palaces dripping with gold, his first splash in public life came at university, when he beat a fellow student to death with a cane in front of hundreds for not showing him sufficient respect. Amnesty reports describe him torturing athletes who lost matches: ordering their legs broken, locking them in prison or forcing them to kick concrete footballs until their feet shattered. He abducted women off the street and raped them at their own weddings, and once he shot his father's valet dead at a party.

And then there's Kim Jong-Un. Raised on yachts, ski trips and imported Swiss cheese flown in from Europe, he grew up with Michael Jordan VHS tapes and entourages that bowed at every word. With no checks on his ego, he turned into a modern Caligula. Intelligence reports describe him executing rivals with anti-aircraft guns, feeding his uncle to dogs and having various officials incinerated with flamethrowers. He has built over a dozen palaces while presiding over famines that starve tens of thousands.

None of these men were born monsters. They became them by being pampered from birth. Because if you've never felt pain, you can't recognise it in others. If you've never hauled your own emotional boulder up a hill, you assume anyone at the bottom is just slacking off. That's why sadness matters. It's a built-in failsafe – a psychological rumble strip that slows down our worst instincts.

It's why your wisest, warmest and most emotionally fluent friends aren't the ones with the perfect teeth and a happening rack. They're the ones who've had their boulder roll away and who slowly, stubbornly, rolled it back. They know when to talk, when to hug, when to crack a joke and when to just sit next to you and let it rain.

So the next time you're miserable, just remember that pain is doing its job. It's sanding down your ego and deepening your empathy.

Sociopaths may not get depressed, but they also don't get invited to dinner.

Misery Can Make You Calmer

Have you seen *Good Will Hunting*? If not, you should. It's good. Matt Damon plays Will Hunting, a working-class maths prodigy who can solve all sorts of squiggly sums in his sleep but can't talk about his feelings without punching a wall. Trauma, abandonment, anger, attachment issues – they're all bubbling away under the surface, buried beneath a thick Boston accent and three layers of flannel.

Enter Sean, a therapist played by Robin Williams, and a man who's clearly known grief. Session after session, they dance around Will's problems, as he deflects every question with a joke or a threat. But then, in the film's most famous scene, Sean simply says, 'It's not your fault.' Again. And again. Until Will finally breaks down and sobs.

That's the moment that changes everything. That's the moment when Will's new life begins.

Because for all its bad PR, crying is one of the most elegant biological coping systems we've got. Emotional tears biochemically expel sadness. They're loaded with stress hormones and prolactin, meaning every sob is your nervous system wringing out cortisol like a hormonal dishcloth. Put simply, you're releasing pressure.

In a 2008 study led by psychologist Jonathan Rottenberg at the University of South Florida, 88.8 per cent of people reported feeling noticeably better after crying, as long as they weren't being judged, shamed or interrupted mid-sob by a barista asking if they wanted oat milk. Context matters. But the catharsis? That's legit.

And the perks of sadness don't stop at tear ducts. Psychologist George Bonanno of Columbia University, who's spent decades studying grief and emotional resilience, found that people who acknowledge their emotional pain recover faster and more fully from loss. They let sadness move through them like a storm, letting it roll in and soak them. Then, eventually, it passes. And the grass grows greener.

As Lisa Feldman Barrett, one of the world's leading emotion researchers, observes, 'Emotions are not problems to be solved. They are signals to be interpreted.' Your anxiety isn't weakness. Your tears aren't failure. They're just your brain waving a tiny orange flag and saying, 'Pull over. Take a break. Stretch your legs.'

Crying is maintenance. It's your nervous system venting steam before the engine blows. It's emotional plumbing. It's you not becoming Caligula. Sadness – like rain – waters the roots and makes things grow.

So next time you cry, don't apologise. You're rinsing the windscreen so you can see the road again. And when the skies clear, step outside. The world always smells better after rain.

Misery Can Make You Smarter

I have a dog who is just relentlessly cheerful. I'm talking non-stop tail wags, incessant cuddles and constant attempts to make friends. It doesn't matter if the 'friend' is a bee, a cat that wants to kill him or an oncoming car. He is wholesome. Sweet. Adorable.

And, needless to say, a complete idiot. For all its undoubted surface appeal, unfiltered happiness does not sharpen the brain. Chronically cheerful people are more likely to trust their gut, ignore red flags or fall for shiny distractions. (And if my dog is any guide, it may well be that they eat their own poo.)

Sadness, by contrast, slows us down. It makes us think. It tells us to read the fine print, Google the side effects and maybe not get in a white van with a stranger. It's what teaches us to not buy sushi from a service station, or send money to that Nigerian price. It's the voice in our head that says 'don't text your ex'.

Studies in affective neuroscience and social psychology show that low mood improves focus, accuracy and lie detection. When we're sad, we actually pay attention. We fact-check. We look beneath the surface. One study in *Emotion* found that people in a slightly sad state were more effective at spotting deception, while another showed that sadness improves memory recall and argument quality, and reduces gullibility. As the study's author put it, 'Sadness is not just a symptom. It's a tool.'

That tool clears the fog. It shuts down the party playlist and switches your brain to serious mode – with better judgement, sharper attention to detail and a much lower risk of believing Chad is emotionally available just because he has abs and long, blonde, floofy hair.

Proust, who knew his way around melancholy, put it more elegantly: 'Happiness is beneficial for the body, but it is grief that develops the powers of the mind.' Or, less poetically: sadness is your internal BS filter. It installs a pop-up blocker for toxic optimism. It makes you a little more sceptical, a little more grounded – and a lot less likely to buy an NFT.

Psychologist Joseph Forgas at the University of New South Wales found that people in mildly sad moods process information more carefully and notice more details. In one famous experiment, he piped gloomy music into a shop and customers later recalled up to four times more about the random knick-knacks at the counter.

The upshot? A little gloom sharpens the mind. It boosts attention to detail, strengthens memory, improves critical thinking – and stops us from bounding into danger with wagging tails and big goofy grins.

The world is full of people whose greatness didn't happen *despite* their misery but *because* of it.

Take Charles Darwin. He didn't just stroll off the *Beagle* and toss out *On the Origin of Species*. He spent decades crippled by anxiety, stomach pain, heart palpitations and psychosomatic illness so relentless that one biographer called him 'the most sickly great man who ever lived'. Darwin often wrote letters fretting about his 'nervous weakness' and lived most of his life as a recluse in Kent. But illness gave him what London dinner parties never could: silence, solitude and the obsessive focus to stare at barnacles for eight years straight. His sickness was a cocoon, and out of it crawled evolution.

Or Isaac Newton, possibly the grumpiest genius in history. He once jabbed a needle behind his own eye just to see what would happen, and he wrestled with depression, paranoia and rage. Yet in the long silences when he shut himself away from society, Newton didn't just sulk – he discovered gravity, invented calculus and reframed the universe. He didn't launch the Enlightenment because he was cheerful. He did it because he couldn't stop thinking and no one else was very keen to hang out.

Then there's Stephen Hawking. Diagnosed with motor neurone disease at 21, he was given two years to live by doctors. Instead, he lived another five decades, wrote *A Brief History of Time* and turned the cosmos into a household conversation topic. He spent most of his life in a wheelchair, communicating through a speech synthesiser, yet said, 'My disability has not been a serious handicap in my scientific work. In some ways, it has been an advantage.' Trapped in his body, misery didn't stop him. It gave him focus.

So next time you're stuck in a slump, you may not be stuck at all. You're learning and thinking about life. You're becoming a person with something to say.

Misery Can Make You More Creative

The Beach Boys sang about surfing, cars and 'Good Vibrations' – but one of them hadn't left the house in years. While the rest of the band was having fun, fun, fun, Brian Wilson was holed up in his bedroom, battling panic attacks, hallucinations, depression and drug addiction.

Here's the twist: he didn't write great songs in spite of that suffering. He wrote them because of it. 'Pain is what makes music great,' Wilson said. 'If you're feeling good, you're not gonna write anything deep.' He added, 'Music is God's voice. But it comes out better when you're hurting.'

And he's not the only one. Lady Gaga put it plainly: 'Some of the most painful moments of my life have turned into some of the most powerful music I've ever made.' And the evidence suggests that she's far from alone. Just look at the roll call: Amy Winehouse, gone from alcohol poisoning in 2011. Kurt Cobain, suicide in 1994. Jimi Hendrix, overdose in 1970. Janis Joplin, heroin the same year. Jim Morrison, collapsed in a Paris bathtub in 1971. Brian Jones, Rolling Stones founder, drowned in his pool in 1969. All shooting stars that burned out early. And that's just the ones who died at 27.

There's a pattern here that's hard to miss: misery has been the great muse of modern music. Even when it didn't kill the musicians, it gave their songs a strange, almost sacred weight. Misery doesn't just haunt the margins of art. It more or less writes the chorus.

And it's not just musicians. That's the awkward truth about genius: suffering isn't just endured, it's recycled. Pain gets turned into poetry. Heartbreak into symphonies. Loneliness into canvases. Great art comes out of the furnace. Comfort, meanwhile, just lounges in a hammock eating grapes – lovely to live with, useless in the studio.

If emotional pain were a sport, artists of every stripe would be bringing home the gold. The training regime? Sleepless nights, broken hearts and years of feeling like an outsider at the party. You don't create masterpieces from a comfy house in the suburbs, built on stable relationships and a nice steady job. Art doesn't come from contentment – from feeling tickety-boo and A-OK while you mow the lawn and baste the Sunday roast. Great art doesn't come from being relaxed; it comes from being rattled. From longing, from heartbreak, from resentment, from dread. From the creeping (albeit drug-addled) realisation that one of your shoes may, in fact, be alive.

That's why the 'tortured artist' stereotype is so enduring: the rock star trashing hotel rooms; the poet hunched over a notebook, chain-smoking like it's a competitive sport; the painter freezing in a Paris garret. The bohemian starter pack has never been smug stability; it's empty bottles and unpaid rent.

Aristotle saw it coming: 'All men who have attained excellence ... have a melancholic habitus.' Nietzsche just shouted it louder: 'One must still have chaos in oneself to give birth to a dancing star.'

And if you want further proof, you don't have to look far. Forget the rock stars for a moment, writers have been running the misery marathon since the dawn of time. They practically invented the tortured-artist cliché. Virginia Woolf channelled her turmoil into prose of huge psychological depth. But the same mind that invented stream-of-consciousness also pulled her into rivers of despair: in 1941 she filled her pockets with stones and walked into the Ouse.

Franz Kafka spent his days as an anxious insurance clerk and his nights turning dread into fiction. *The Trial* and *The Metamorphosis* weren't wild inventions – they were mirrors of his own paralysis and fear.

Tennessee Williams, haunted by depression, addiction and a sister lobotomised at 33, poured it into *A Streetcar Named Desire* and *The Glass Menagerie*. His characters unravelled because he did too.

Sylvia Plath turned anguish into dazzling but devastating verse. She wrote *Ariel* in a burst of manic energy before ending her life in 1963, aged 30.

Ernest Hemingway described writing as 'sitting at a typewriter and bleeding'. His pared-back style came from war trauma, depression and alcohol. Eventually, he bled literally, shooting himself in 1961.

None of them escaped misery. They wrote from inside it.

And what about painters? Vincent van Gogh cut off part of his ear after a fight with Gauguin, checked himself into asylums and, in just ten years, produced over 2000 works. He shot himself in 1890, at 37, leaving behind canvases that turned private torment into universal colour.

Frida Kahlo, shattered in a bus crash at 18, lived with pain, operations and betrayal. From her bed, she painted fierce self-portraits – unibrow proud, body broken but spirit blazing. 'The Broken Column' and 'Henry Ford Hospital' turned suffering into art.

Mark Rothko painted mood itself. His vast colour fields became sacred spaces for viewers, while he slid deeper into depression. In 1970, he killed himself in his New York studio, leaving behind walls drenched in both paint and grief.

The lesson is simple. Great artists don't wait for peace. They take suffering and turn it into material.

So if your life feels messy, maybe that's not the worst thing. That's the raw material. Grab a pen. Pick up a brush. Sit at the piano. Scream into the void. And see if you can turn the mess into gold.

24

LET IT BE

Why this book can be judged by its cover

Happiness is like a butterfly; the more you
chase it, the more it will elude you.
Robert Lee, *The Night Thoreau spent in Jail*, 1970

People love to say 'You can't judge a book by its cover'. But, let's be honest, people say a lot of things.

'The Moon landing was fake.'

'I'm voting Trump.'

'Israel's bombing raid was targeted and proportionate.'

The truth is, book covers – and their titles – matter. A lot. Which is why I spent a slightly embarrassing amount of time over mine. Some of the titles I threw around included: *Much Too Great Expectations*, *Be Your Worst Self*, *Good Grief*, *The Power of Negative Thinking*, *The Joy of Sadness*, *The Pursuit of Unhappiness*, *Suck It Up*, *Don't Hang in There*, *Woe Is Us* and *Up in the Dumps*.

Ultimately, however, I realised they all sucked. And maybe *The Importance of Being Miserable* kind of sucks too.

But whatever you think of the title, I hope the message sticks. Because being miserable is quite important. Today's obsession with happiness is a cultural anomaly, a strange, modern quirk that's completely out of sync with how humans have always thought. Thousands of generations before us never expected life to be easy or fulfilling or even particularly enjoyable. They simply assumed that suffering was part of the deal.

And, of course, there's every reason to think that they were happier for it. When you expect life to be tough, every moment of joy feels like a win. When you accept that suffering is inevitable, you stop wasting energy fighting it. When you don't demand constant happiness, you're far less disappointed when it doesn't arrive.

This doesn't mean we should all go back to living in caves or renounce modern comforts in some kind of grand philosophical protest. But it does mean we should take a step back and reassess what we've been conditioned to believe. Feeling good isn't everything. And feeling bad isn't the end of the world. You don't need to panic every time you're sad. You don't need to 'fix' every bad mood. You don't need to assume that an imperfect life is a failed one.

Instead, take some solace in the wisdom of the ages. For most of history, people accepted that life wasn't meant to be perfect, that emotions weren't meant to be constant, that struggle, sadness and suffering weren't problems to be solved. They were simply part of what it means to be alive.

So the next time you're feeling down, don't reach for a self-help book or a motivational podcast. Don't spiral into self-doubt about whether you're doing life wrong. Just sit with it. Accept it. Treat it like the weather.

Happiness is not a full-time job. It's not a goal, a project or a life requirement. It's just something that happens from time to time. And when it does? Great. Enjoy it. But when it doesn't? That's fine, too. Sadness isn't the end of happiness. It's the beginning of meaning. Come what may, you'll probably get through it. Just like every generation before you.

They say that misery loves company. So congratulations: you've joined a large club.